JANUARY

Make the Most of Every Month with Carson-Dellosa's Monthly Books!

Production Manager
Chris McIntyre

Editorial Director
Jennifer Weaver-Spencer

Writers
Lynette Pyne
Amy Gamble
Danielle Schultz

Editors
Maria McKinney
Kelly Gunzenhauser
Carol Layton
Tracy Soles

Art Directors
Alain Barsony
Penny Casto

Illustrators
Mike Duggins
Edward Fields
Erik Huffine
David Lackey
Ray Lambert
Bill Neville
Betsy Peninger
J.J. Rudisill
Pam Thayer
Todd Tyson
Julie Webb

Cover Design
Amber Kocher Crouch
Ray Lambert
J.J. Rudisill

D1372038

Carson-Dellosa Publishing Company, Inc.

JANUARY

Table of Contents

JANUARY TEACHER TIPS

Answer Cards

Use answer cards to tell which student need extra help. Give each student 18 index cards. Have each child create a set of cards for multiple choice questions by programming cards with the letters *A*, *B*, *C*, and *D*. Check math facts by making a set of math cards programmed with numbers 0-9. Write *true*, *false*, *yes*, and *no* on the remaining cards. Test the class by asking a question and allowing time for students to find the correct card. On your signal, have each student hold up his card.

Winter Recess Fun

Cure the wintertime blues by making a batch of playdough for students to use during indoor recess. Mix 1 cup flour, $\frac{1}{4}$ cup salt, 1 teaspoon vegetable oil, and several drops of food coloring. Pour wet ingredients into a saucepan and mix with dry ingredients. Cook all ingredients over medium heat until mixture reaches a dough consistency. Remove from heat and allow dough to cool completely. Store in an airtight container.

Quick Check

Know at a glance which student papers need to be checked and which can be returned. Label a clothespin *Check* and another *Return*. Use the *Check* clothespin to clip together all papers that need to be graded. Use the *Return* clothespin to clip together all papers that have been graded and are ready to be returned to students.

Indoor Snowballs

Make yarn snowballs for students to play with during any season. Using a skein of white yarn, wrap a continuous length around the palm of your hand until it forms a large bundle. Carefully slide the bundle off your hand. Tie a short piece of yarn around the center of the bundle. Cut the looped edges on both ends of the bundle and pull the ends toward the center to make a pompom.

Winter Clothesline

Put an end to missing mittens and scarves using a winter clothesline. Suspend a length of heavy string along a classroom wall. Label clothespins with student names. Instruct each student to clip her mittens and scarf on the clothesline using the clothespin labeled with her name.

Organize Stickers

Locate holiday and seasonal stickers quickly. Label dividers in a small accordion folder with the names of holidays and seasons. Place stickers related to each topic in the appropriate pockets.

January

1 **New Year's Day** Have a class discussion about newsworthy events of the past year.

2 **National Reaching Your Potential Month** Create an *I Can* bulletin board. Cut out construction paper exclamation marks. Have students write three things they can do on the stems of the exclamation marks and their names on the points. Post on a bulletin board.

3 **Alaska became the 49th state** today in 1959. Have students find Alaska on a map and name its capital.

JUNEAU

4 **New Year's Resolution Week** is January 4-8. Have students share their New Year's resolutions with the class.

5 **National Book Month** Keep a list of books students read this month on chart paper. Display the list on the wall and see who reads the most.

6 **Universal Letter Writing Week** is January 7-10. Make stationery with the class and have students use it to write a letter to a family member or friend.

MAIL

SPECIAL DELIVERY

7 **National Hobby Month** Take a poll to see what hobbies are most popular. Graph the results.

4

Day-by-Day Calendar

8 **Elvis Presley's Birthday** The performer was born today in 1935. Bring in a recording of his music to share with the class.

9 **Adopt-a-Dog Month** Invite students to make posters encouraging people to adopt a dog from a shelter.

10 **National Eye Care Month** Have an optometrist visit and tell the class about eye care.

11 **National Clean-Off-Your-Desk Day** Take some time out and let students clean their desks, inside and out.

12 **Pandas** were **added to the endangered species list** on this day in 1985. Have students research other endangered animals and brainstorm a list of ways to help save them.

PROTECT THE PANDAS!

13 **Michael Bond's Birthday** The author of the Paddington Bear™ stories was born today in 1926. Share a Paddington story with the class.

14 **Secret Pal Day** Put students' names in a hat. Have each student draw a name without telling who it is. Let students do something nice for their secret pals, such as draw a picture, write a nice letter, etc. Allot some time at the end of the day for students to reveal their secret pals.

15 **Martin Luther King, Jr.'s Birthday** The civil rights leader was born today in 1929. Have students write their dreams for a better world and share them with the class.

16 *National Nothing Day* was created "to provide Americans with one national day when they can just sit without celebrating or honoring anything." Have students draw symbols for National Nothing Day.

17  *Benjamin Franklin's Birthday* He was born today in 1706. Talk with students about his experiments with electricity. Let them create static electricity by rubbing balloons in their hair.

18 The *snowdrop is the January flower*. Ask students to fold a piece of drawing paper in half. On one side, have them draw a picture of what they think a snowdrop looks like. Then, share a picture of a snowdrop. On the other side of the paper, have students draw a picture of what the flower actually looks like.

19 *Edgar Allen Poe's Birthday* The author was born on this day in 1809. Brainstorm a list of things that make a story scary. Then, have students write their own scary stories.

20 *Edwin "Buzz" Aldrin's Birthday* The astronaut was born today in 1930. Tell the class that he was aboard Apollo 11 which flew the first men to the moon. Let children do moon walk dances in his honor.

21 *National Hugging Day*™ Have students create hug certificates for special people in their lives.

22 *National High-Tech Month* Brainstorm a list of machines that make our lives easier.

23 *National Pie Day* Ask students to create their favorite pies from construction paper. Hang the pies on the wall in a bar graph showing the most popular to least popular pies.

24 *Gold* was *discovered at Sutter's Mill California* on this day in 1848. Spray paint small rocks gold. Place several pans of sand, rocks, and water around a table. Provide a strainer or sieve at each station. Bury several of the gold rocks in each container and let students take turns panning for gold.

25 The *first telephone conversation* took place today in 1915. Have students write dialogs as if they were participants in this conversation.

26 *Mary Mapes Dodge's Birthday* The children's author was born today in 1831. Read a chapter from *Hans Brinker and the Silver Skates* to celebrate.

27 *Lewis Carroll's Birthday* The *Alice in Wonderland* author was born today in 1832. Let students create a "weird" world, their version of what it looks like "beyond the looking glass."

28 *Oatmeal Month* Have students come up with new flavors for this breakfast favorite. Then, have them write ads promoting their new flavors.

29 *National Puzzle Day* Let students solve a puzzle in honor of this day.

30 *Reminiscence Month* Have students write and illustrate a journal entry on one of their favorite memories.

31 *Scotch*® *Tape* was *developed* on this day in 1928. Have students brainstorm a list for all its uses.

5

Sunday	Monday	Tuesday	Wednesday	Thursday	Friday	Saturday

January

January Gazette

Teacher _____ Date _____

IN THE NEWS

← TAKE NOTE   WHAT'S COMING UP →

KID'S CORNER

cold	i	c	o	l	d	n
ice	s	c	u	q	e	l
icicle	n	z	i	t	u	i
mitten	o	i	t	c	l	c
sled	w	i	m	z	l	e
snow	m	s	l	e	d	e

7

Celebrate January!

Dear Family Members,
Here are a few quick-and-easy activities to help you and your child celebrate special days throughout the month of January.

January 1 is *New Year's Day*
- Talk with your child about memorable events from the past year. What was the best thing that happened? What events will you remember in the years to come? Write a short paragraph detailing the events and seal it in a clean 16-ounce soda bottle. Save the bottle to open next New Year's day.

January is *National Hobby Month*
- Find a hobby that interests you and your child that you can enjoy together. Hobbies might include playing sports, collecting stamps, identifying birds, cooking, etc.

January 23 is *National Pie Day*
- Make miniature pies using frozen tartlet shells. Fill each shell halfway with your favorite prepared pie filling. Bake the tartlets according to the pie filling package instructions.

January 25 is *the anniversary of the first telephone conversation,* in 1915.
- Have your child practice the correct way to answer the telephone and teach him or her to take phone messages. If your child does not already know your phone number, help him or her learn it. Also, teach your child to dial 911 in an emergency.

January is *Oatmeal Month*
- Make and enjoy these oatmeal cookies with your child.
  - 1 cup chocolate chips
  - 3-4 tablespoons peanut butter, optional
  - 3 cups oatmeal
  - 1 teaspoon vanilla extract
  - 1 stick margarine
  - $1/2$ cup milk
  - 2 cups sugar

Place chocolate chips, peanut butter, oatmeal, and vanilla in a large mixing bowl. Combine the margarine, milk, and sugar in a saucepan; bring to a rolling boil. Boil for one minute. Combine the hot mixture with the oatmeal mixture; stir well. Drop by spoonfuls on waxed paper. Makes approximately two dozen cookies.

January 29 is *National Puzzle Day*
- Help your child make a jigsaw puzzle. Have your child draw and color a picture, then glue it to a piece of poster board. Cut the picture into several pieces. Take turns putting the puzzle together.

Read In January!

Dear Family Members,
Here are some books to share with your child to enhance the enjoyment of reading in January.

First Night by Harriet Ziefert
- *A little girl gets to lead the New Year parade at a First Night celebration.*
- Make decorations and noise makers with your child and let him or her lead a New Year parade through the house.

Sam and the Lucky Money by Karen Chinn
- *Sam is having a hard time deciding how to spend the four dollars of "lucky money" he received for Chinese New Year. Instead of spending it on himself, he gives the money to a homeless man in need.*
- After reading the story, discuss the saying, "It is better to give than to receive." Encourage your child to describe a time when he or she gave a special gift and how it felt to give it.

My Dream of Martin Luther King by Faith Ringgold
- *The author recounts a dream she had about Martin Luther King, Jr., which includes major events of his life and the Civil Rights Movement.*
- After reading the book, discuss with your child why it is important to treat everyone fairly and solve problems peacefully. Brainstorm ways to resolve conflicts.

The Biggest, Best Snowman by Margery Cuyler
- *Nell's family tells her she is too small to help them so she builds a big snowman and shows them that even small people can do big things!*
- Help your child come up with a list of things he or she can do to help out at home even though he or she may be smaller than others in the family.

Snow Dance by Lezlie Evans
- *Several children enjoy playing in all of the snow that falls as a result of their snow dance. Rhyming, rhythmic text makes this snowy story a fun read-aloud.*
- Let the creative juices flow and make it snow! Make up a snow dance with your child using the snowflake-like movements (swirling, twirling, etc.) mentioned in the book. You may wish to read the book in a rhythmic, song-like way while your child performs the snow dance.

Millions of Snowflakes by Mary McKenna Siddals
- *Simple, rhyming text and playful illustrations capture a little girl's joy as she plays in the snow and counts the snowflakes falling from the sky.*
- Have your child read this simple book to you. Then, review the illustrations together and count the number of snowflake pictures throughout the book.

You are Unique

because _____

Name _____

Signed _____

Date _____

YOUR PROGRESS IS SPEEDING RIGHT ALONG!

Name _____

Subject _____

Signed _____

Date _____

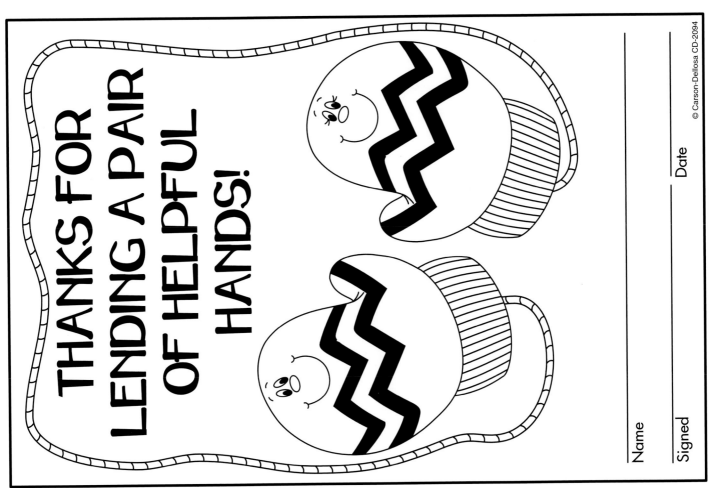

THANKS FOR LENDING A PAIR OF HELPFUL HANDS!

Name _____

Signed _____ Date _____

COOL WORK

Name _____

Signed _____ Date _____

JANUARY Writing Activities

What do new beginnings, snowflakes, and wintry weather have in common? They all occur in January! These "cool" ideas are sure to have your students writing up a storm!

Shape up for Spelling

Help students remember the letters in a word by pointing out the shape of the word. Ascenders and descenders (or the absence of them) give a word a unique shape that can be used as a cue to recognizing the correct spelling. After students have written their spelling lists for the week, have them trace around each word and note the shape.

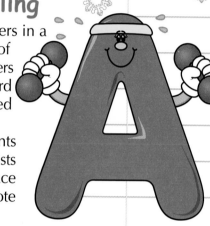

Subject Jars

Make a subject jar for quick descriptive writing exercises. Write wintry subjects, such as chicken noodle soup, polar bear, snowman, etc., on slips of paper and place them in a jar. Let students pull subjects from the jar and write paragraphs using as many senses as possible to describe the objects. Have each student read his paragraph while the others try to guess what the object is.

Word Bank Words

snowflake	icicle
snowman	mittens
scarf	shiver
boots	chilly
ski	frozen
cocoa	winter
sled	ice skate

Guess What Happened to Me?!

The new year gets people thinking about what they did not complete during the last year. Make these new year reflections more positive by having students write a narrative about the best thing that happened to them in the last year. Let students share their experiences in small groups and vote on whose experience was best.

It's a Snow Day!

What if today was a snow day? This may be a real or imagined possibility for your area, but either way, students will enjoy writing about creative and fun ways to spend a day off from school.

Let it Snow, Let it Snow, Let it Snow

Mother Nature is unpredictable in the winter. Sometimes she sends lots of snow and sometimes none at all. Have students write to Mother Nature asking for certain types of weather. Let students give reasons in their letters for their requests and include polite thank-yous for Mother Nature's time.

Snowy Poems

Encourage students to use figurative language in their poetry. Look outside at objects covered with snow and ice (or look at a snowy scene in a picture). Instead of describing the snow as *white* or *pretty*, have students think about what an object covered with snow looks like. For example, a bush covered in snow may look like a cupcake frosted with fresh whipped cream. Have students write snowy poems so that each line describes the landscape topped off with snow.

> Gingerbread houses with stiff white icing.
> Cupcake bushes nearby topped with fresh
>   whipped cream.
> Marshmallow fluff sticks to my boots.
> Chilled chocolate branches dusted with
>   powdered sugar.
> Winter makes me hungry!

What Would a Snowflake Say?

Imagine whirling, twirling, and dancing to Earth from an icy snow cloud high in the sky. Have students write snowflake adventure stories that tell about the journey a snowflake makes from cloud to ground. Students can choose to write their stories in first person, as if they are the snowflakes, or from another perspective, such as a narrator, a bird, a cloud, etc.

Positively Editing

When students are editing each others' stories, they often just point out things that are wrong. This can create negative feelings about writing and revising and can cause students to become discouraged. One way to make the editing process more pleasant and criticism more easily accepted is to have students begin and end their editorial comments on a positive note. Students may say they enjoyed the story or that a particular part was funny.

13

Bulletin Board Ideas

Start the New Year off right with this display. Enlarge the Baby New Year and clock patterns (pages 34-35) and post them on the bulletin board. Let each student make a noisemaker by tracing and cutting out two handprints. On one hand print, have each student write his name, and on the other, a resolution for the new year. Glue the handprints to the end of a cone shape cut from construction paper to make a noisemaker. This display complements the *New Year Throughout the World* chapter (pages 20-35).

Use this display to welcome the Chinese New Year. Cover a bulletin board with blue paper. Decorate the board with student-made crafts from the Chinese New Year section (pages 25-26) of the *New Year Throughout the World* chapter (pages 20-35). Display firecrackers, scrolls, lucky money packets, lion masks, paper pictures, and dancing dragons.

14

WINTER WONDERLAND!

Anna

Teri

Tim

Haley

Edward

Denise

Create a cheery wintry weather scene complete with snowmen. Cover a bulletin board with dark blue paper. Use cotton batting to create snow drifts and cut out snowflakes to create a border. Have students decorate and cut out copies of the snowman pattern (page 54) and display them on the bulletin board. Children can tear small pieces of white paper to attach to the display to create snowflakes. This display corresponds to the *Let it Snow!* chapter (pages 46-55).

FROSTY FUN

Sara
Lisa
Jeff
Claire
Tommy
Andre
JULIE
Kenny
Angela

Create some snowy day fun with this display. Cover the top of a bulletin board with blue paper and make a large snow bank from white paper. Cut icicles from aluminum foil and place them on the top and bottom of the board. Add snow-covered trees to the background. Cut a pond from aluminum foil and attach it to the bulletin board. Have students draw and cut out self-portraits on white paper showing them involved in their favorite wintertime activities. Post the completed pictures on the bulletin board. Display this bulletin board with the *Let it Snow!* chapter (pages 46-55).

15

Highlight students' creative writing abilities with this idea. Decorate the bulletin board to look like a $100 bill. Let students draw a picture of Benjamin Franklin on a green circle of construction paper and place it on the board, slightly off-center. Have each student draw and cut out a $100 bill with her face in the center. Post each student's bill with a paragraph explaining what she could do to get her face on the $100 bill. This display works well with the *Benjamin Franklin* chapter (pages 84-88).

Honor the work of Dr. Martin Luther King, Jr. with a display focusing on his life. Enlarge the Martin Luther King, Jr. pattern (page 69) and place it in the middle of the bulletin board. Using the time line on page 65, write each event on a sentence strip. Have volunteers draw pictures on circles of construction paper to go with the events. Place the circles around the pattern in order, using arrows. If desired, mix up the events and challenge students to put them in order. Use this bulletin board idea with the *Honoring Dr. Martin Luther King, Jr.* chapter (pages 65-69).

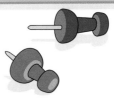

Turn your students into storytellers with this display. Cover the top of a bulletin board with light blue paper. Create a landscape with green paper. Cut out rectangles and triangles from gray paper and put them together to resemble castles. Add flags to the castles. Have each student design a book cover and write a synopsis of his favorite fairy tale. Post the book covers on the castles. Use this display with the *Once Upon a Time* chapter (pages 70-79).

This informative display will help students learn about the Inuit and Sami. Divide the bulletin board into two sections with a paper banner that reads *People of the Arctic*. Label one section *Inuit* and the other *Sami*. Cut out colorful squares from construction paper to create a border that resembles a Sami design. Attach Inuit snowhouses and Sami hats, bonnets, and kåtas (pages 81-82) under the correct sections. This display complements the *People of the Arctic* chapter (pages 80-83).

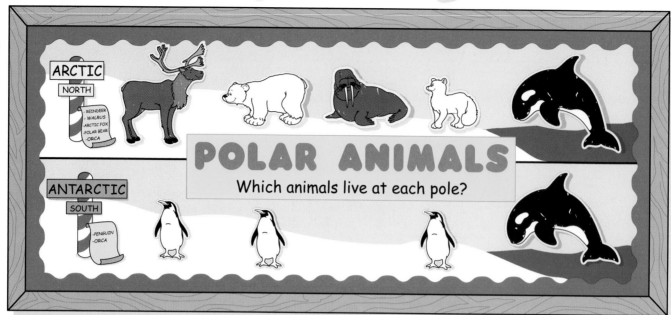

Use this display to teach children about Arctic and Antarctic animals. Cover a bulletin board with blue paper. Divide it into two sections, labeling one *Arctic (North)* and the other *Antarctic (South)*. Add a snow bank to each section. Have students color and cut out the polar bear, reindeer, arctic fox, walrus, orca, and Emperor penguin patterns (pages 62-64) and place each animal in its appropriate habitat. Add a list of animals that can be found in each region to each section. This display corresponds to the *Polar Animals* chapter (pages 56-64).

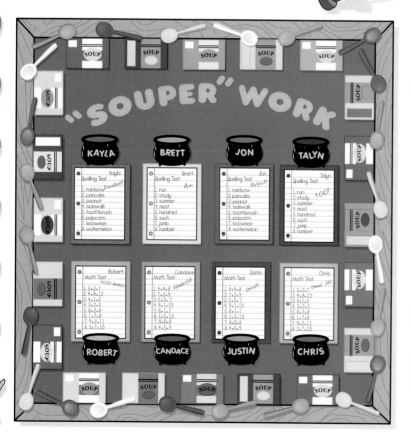

Spotlight student work with this piping hot display. Cover a bulletin board with green paper and give each child a copy of the soup kettle pattern (page 38) to cut out. Provide alphabet shaped pasta noodles for students to spell their names on their soup kettles. Accent great student work using the soup kettles. Create a border by attaching soup labels and plastic spoons around the display. This bulletin board idea works well with the *Soup's On!* chapter (pages 36-38).

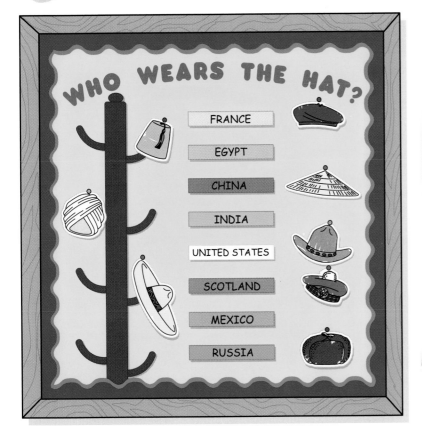

WHO WEARS THE HAT?

FRANCE

EGYPT

CHINA

INDIA

UNITED STATES

SCOTLAND

MEXICO

RUSSIA

Find out who wears the hat! Cover a bulletin board with yellow paper. Cut a hat rack shape from brown construction paper and place it on the left side of the board. Enlarge the hat patterns (page 91) and place one on each peg of the rack. On sentence strips, write the names of countries where each hat can be found and place them on the board. Challenge students to match each hat to its country by placing the pattern beside the correct sentence strip. This display works well with the *Hats Off to Hats* chapter (pages 89-92).

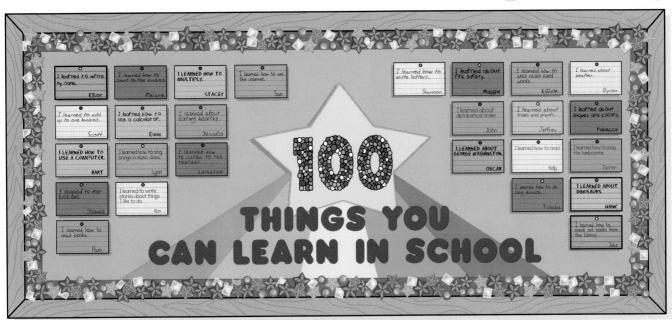

The more students learn, the more items they can add to this display. Cut a large 100 from poster board. Have students cover the pattern with small items such as jelly beans or buttons. Cut a large star shape from yellow construction paper and attach the 100 to it. Then, place the star in the center of the board. Use colorful strips of paper to create a rainbow effect below the star. Add a border of items and have students count out the items as they are being glued to the board. Provide colorful index cards and have the class write 100 things they learned in school. Post the cards around the 100. Use this display during your study of the *100th Day Celebration* chapter (pages 39-43).

New Year Throughout the World

People of many nationalities and religions observe New Year. The beginning of a new year marks a time for celebration, reflection, and relaxation in many countries. Learn how other cultures celebrate this festive holiday.

Did You Know?

* January was named for the Roman god, Janus, who had two faces so he could look back at the last year and forward at the year to come at the same time.

* The image of the New Year as a baby probably came from the ancient Greeks. The Greeks celebrated the New Year in the spring and honored Dionysus, the god of the vine, who, portrayed as a baby, symbolized the renewal of life in spring.

* Some cultures celebrate the new year in the spring or fall, as their calendars are based on the moon's cycles and not on the Earth's position in relation to the sun, like the western calendar.

Literature Selections

Happy New Year by Emery Bernhard: Lodestar Books, 1996. (Informative book, 32 pg.) An in-depth look at how people all over the word, in ancient times, and in the present, celebrate the New Year.

First Night by Harriet Ziefert: Putnam Publishing Group, 1999. (Picture book, 32 pg.) A little girl gets to lead the New Year parade at a First Night celebration.

Dumpling Soup by Jama Kim Rattigan: Little Brown & Co., 1998. (Picture book, 32 pg.) A girl in Hawaii gets to help make the New Year dumplings as she celebrates the holiday with her culturally diverse family.

Create a Whole New Year

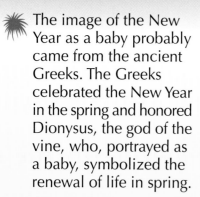

In many cultures, displaying a new calendar is an important part of the New Year. Students can make their own New Year calendars. Give each child 12 copies of the calendar grid (page 6). Block out the month name and artwork by taping plain white paper over it before copying. Help children bind the pages together with a spiral book binding machine or by punching three holes along the top and threading yarn through each hole. Let students write each month name at the top of each page. Use a calendar to determine on what day January 1 will fall. Have each student fill in the date on the January page and use the number of days in each month to determine the rest of the calendar. Each student can draw a picture related to each month on the back of the previous month's grid. Draw a picture on a separate sheet of paper for January, then design a cover for the calendar on the other side of that sheet.

New Year In
The United States

Did You Know?

- People in the United States celebrate the New Year with parties, noisemakers, and a ceremonial countdown to midnight. Many people watch a large, lighted ball drop at midnight in Times Square in New York city.
- The tradition of the Tournament of Roses parade in California, followed by a sporting event, dates back to the late 1800s.
- Traditional good luck foods eaten on New Year's Day vary from region to region and include collard greens and black eyed peas, or pork and sauerkraut.

Be a Reporter

In the United States, people celebrate New Year's Eve in different ways. Some people go to parties and others stay home and watch television reports about celebrations in other places. Have students imagine they are newspaper or TV reporters. Their assignment is to cover a New Year's Eve celebration in Times Square, their house, or another place. First, let students share celebrations they have seen. Talk about all the people, the parties, the music, etc. Then, have students write out their reports and post them on a bulletin board. If desired, let students act out television broadcasts of their New Year's Eve reports.

Countdown to Midnight 3, 2, 1...

Watching the clock and counting down to midnight is a popular New Year tradition. To get ready for New Year's Eve, have students practice telling how long it is until midnight. Give each student a clock pattern (page 35) and ask her to draw the hands on the clock to show any time she wishes. Be sure to write a.m. or p.m. on the clock. Display the clocks on a wall or bulletin board and number them. Then, have students number their papers and calculate how long it would take for each clock to reach midnight. Challenge older students to calculate each amount in hours and minutes.

a.m.

16 hours

p.m.

6 hours + 5 minutes

p.m.

9 hours

a.m.

20 hours + 30 minutes

If a Year Could Talk

People often represent the New Year with the image of a baby and the old year as an old man with a long white beard. Have students imagine what might be said between Baby New Year and old Father Time when they meet on New Year's Eve and write a dialog of the conversation. Cut out the Baby New Year and Father Time patterns (page 34), color, and tape unsharpened pencils or craft sticks to the backs to make puppets. Let each child act out his dialog using his puppets.

Time Capsules

The New Year is a time for thinking about the future. Let students imagine their hopes and dreams for the coming year. Have each child write something he hopes will happen at school, at home, with friends, etc., in the new year on notebook paper. Roll the paper into a tube, slide it into a clean dry plastic soda bottle, tighten the cap on the bottle and put some glue around the cap. Keep the bottles sealed inside the time capsule bottles until the end of the school year (or send home for students to open over the summer) then cut them open and see if students' hopes and dreams came true.

Promising Party Hats

The New Year is a time for making resolutions, or promising to make changes for the better. Help students make New Year's resolutions into party hats. 1. Have each student decide what his New Year's resolution will be, cut a large sheet of construction paper into a semicircle, write his resolution on the semicircle and decorate it with markers and glitter. 2. Have each child curl his paper into a cone shape and staple the seams. 3. Gather several short lengths of curling ribbon and tie at one end to form a bunch. Push the ribbon bunch through the hole in the top of the hat and tape inside to secure. 4. To make a chin strap, punch a hole in either side of the hat at the base and tie elastic cord between the holes. Let students wear their resolution hats during *Make Some Noise* (page 23), then staple the hats to a bulletin board for display.

1.

2.

3.

4.

22

Make Some Noise

The U.S., like many other countries around the world, welcomes the New Year with lots of noise. It was once thought that the noise would scare away bad luck and spirits to allow for good luck in the new year. Let children get creative in making their own noisemakers from paper plates, cups, cardboard tubes, or empty tissue boxes. Decorate the container with paper, glitter, sequins, etc., and fill with beans, rice, etc. Seal each noisemaker by taping paper over the openings. Celebrate the new year in class at noon, instead of midnight. Let students count down and use their noisemakers to welcome the New Year.

Confetti Art

Many people in the U.S. throw confetti into the air at midnight on New Year's Eve. Let each student draw a picture of a New Year's Eve scene on construction paper. They may wish to include a clock striking midnight, the ball dropping, or a party scene. Provide confetti, or allow students to cut up bits of paper, or use a hole punch to make their own confetti. Paint a thin layer of watered down glue over the picture and lightly sprinkle with confetti, being careful not to completely cover the picture. Let the glue dry and display the New Year's Eve scenes around the room.

What Time Is It, Baby New Year?

Let students take turns being Baby New Year in this New Year tag game. Choose one student to be Baby New Year and stand with his back turned to the class. Have the other students stand behind a taped-off or drawn line on the opposite side of the classroom. Students ask, "What time is it, Baby New Year?" and Baby New Year responds with a time on the hour, such as "six o' clock." Students can take six steps (one step for each hour) toward Baby New Year. This continues, with each student trying to touch Baby New Year and become the new Baby New Year. If Baby New Year says that it is midnight, he can turn around and chase the other students back to the line. If he catches someone, she becomes the new Baby New Year, if not, play continues.

New Year In China

Did You Know?

- Chinese New Year, also called the Spring Festival, is celebrated on the second new moon following the winter solstice and usually falls in late January or early February. It lasts for fifteen days.
- The Chinese New Year greeting is *Gung Hey Fat Choy,* pronounced phonetically, which means *May you prosper.*
- The holiday centers around happiness and good luck for friends and family. There are many traditions for ensuring good luck in the new year, such as cleaning houses to sweep away bad luck, paying off all debts, buying new clothes, decorating with the color red (a symbol of luck), and placing flowers around the house to symbolize growth.
- Parades with fireworks, paper lanterns, and dancers dressed as lions and dragons are a major part of the celebration.

Literature Selections

Celebrating Chinese New Year by Diane Hoyt-Goldsmith: Holiday House, 1998. (Picture book, 32 pg.) Color photographs accompany a thorough description of the activity surrounding the Chinese New Year celebrations.

Sam and the Lucky Money by Karen Chinn: Lee & Low Books, 1997 (Picture book, 32 pg.) A little boy decides to give his lucky New Year money packets to a homeless man.

The Dancing Dragon by Marcia K. Vaughan: Mondo Publishing, 1996 (Picture book, 24 pg.) Describes the preparations for and celebration of Chinese New Year. Includes a fold-out Chinese dragon.

Animal Personality

The Chinese calendar is organized in a twelve year cycle, in which each year is named for an animal. Chinese legend tells of twelve animals that came to honor Buddha (a figure worshiped in the Buddhist religion). Buddha rewarded the animals by naming a year after each in the order in which they arrived: Rat, Ox, Tiger, Rabbit, Dragon, Snake, Horse, Goat (or Ram), Monkey, Rooster, Dog, and Boar. (The year of a certain animal will have those characteristics as well.) Tell students that the year 2000 is the year of the Dragon and that the years progress forward in a clockwise direction. Give each child a Chinese zodiac pattern (page 35) and have her determine in which animal year she was born. Let each student compare his personality with the animal characteristics and write a paragraph on a separate sheet of paper telling if the description is accurate. If it is not, have him tell which animal is more like him and why.

The Rat

I was born in the year of the rat but I think I have more in common with monkeys than with rats. I don't eat food in trashcans from the floor hopefully people squeal with disgust when they see I am silly like a monkey, I would have much rather been born in that year.

Lucky Money Packet

It is a Chinese New Year tradition for adults to give money to children. Wrapped in red envelopes and decorated with good luck messages, this money is considered lucky. Teach money skills with lucky money packets. Let each student cut out and fold a lucky money packet pattern (page 34) copied on red construction paper. Glue the flaps as shown (right) to form small packets, and write good luck messages on them, such as *May you prosper in the New Year, May you accomplish everything you want this year,* etc. Collect the packets, number them, fill each with a different combination of coin manipulatives (page 35), tape them to secure the flap, and redistribute to students. Have students number a sheet of paper with the number of packets that were made. Let them open each packet, count the coins, and write the amount on their papers beside the corresponding numbers. Pass the packets until each child has seen each packet. Make students feel lucky by giving them a treat for completing the activity. Count the money as a class to help students check their work.

Fold 1 · Fold 2 · Fold 3

Firecrackers

Fireworks are an essential part of a Chinese New Year celebration. A Chinese legend tells about a fierce beast, *Nian* (NEE•an), which also means *year* in Chinese, that terrorized people at the New Year. It was discovered that the beast was afraid of loud noises and the color red, so every new year, people set off fireworks and display red decorations to scare away Nian and any other evil and bad luck. In many places, the fireworks and red decorations have become combined, and people display red firecracker decorations that hang from a string. Students can make their own homemade firecracker decorations. Roll several 4" x 4" squares of red construction paper into small tubes and tape to secure. Punch a hole in one end of each tube and tie a short piece of red yarn in the hole. Make a tassel by knotting several pieces of yarn together. Tie the tassel to the end of a long piece of yarn. Tie a loop at the top of the yarn and tie each of the tubes along the length of the yarn. Hang the "firecrackers" around the room for good luck.

Scroll Poems

In many homes, scrolls of red paper on which good wishes are written are hung during Chinese New Year. Often the good luck messages are written in couplets, a type of poetry that has two lines that usually rhyme and have the same rhythm. Have each child write a good luck couplet on a red paper scroll. Roll each end of a 12" x 18" piece of red construction paper around a long cardboard tube and tape to secure. Roll the paper so it just covers the tube, leaving about six inches of paper in between the rolls. Have each student write a good luck message couplet in the space between the rolls, thread a length of yarn through the top tube, and tie for hanging.

The year is new.
Good luck to you.

– Sarah

Paper Pictures

Many Chinese families decorate their homes with elaborate cut paper pictures during New Year. Students can explore symmetry while making their own paper pictures. Let each student fold a sheet of white paper in half and draw a design that extends from the fold. Cut out the design and open the paper to reveal a symmetrical picture. Glue the cut paper to red construction paper to show off the design, and display around the classroom.

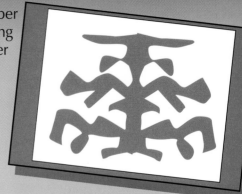

Dancing Dragons

In China, dragons are symbols of strength and prosperity. Traditionally, on the last day of Chinese New Year, a large dancing dragon leads a special lantern parade. Each child can make his own dancing dragon from a small paper cup, a straw, red and white construction paper, red crepe paper streamers, glue, and markers. Have students cut out a red paper tongue and glue it inside the cup so that most of it "hangs" out. Next, have children cut small triangle-shaped "teeth" from white paper and glue them to the inside rims of the cups so they stick out from the cups. Then, allow students to cut out and glue eyes on the outsides of the cups. Glue crepe paper streamers to the back of each cup so they "flow" behind the dragon. Last, tape a straw to the bottom of the cup. Students can hold the straws and wave the dragons, letting the streamers trail behind.

Lion Masks

The *Lion Dance* is a main feature of Chinese New Year parades. Martial artists dress in lion costumes and dance through the streets. They can make the lions' eyes blink and light up with levers inside the lion heads. The lions, in addition to the dragon, serve to scare away bad luck. The lion costumes are decorated with bright colors, feathers, pom-poms, and intricate designs. Let students design their own Chinese lion masks from paper bags. Cut a small slit along the side folds of a paper grocery bag. Place the bag over a child's head and draw circles on the front where the eyes should be cut out. Let each student cut out the eye holes and decorate his lion head with feathers, felt, pom-poms, buttons, paint, and other craft supplies. Challenge students to make up lion dances to perform while wearing their masks.

26

New Year In Japan

Did You Know?

- *Gantan* (GAHN•tahn) is the name for the Japanese New Year, celebrated on January 1. It means *first day of the first month*.
- There are many things the Japanese do to ensure good luck in the new year. They clean their homes, pay off debts, buy new clothes, and decorate with *kadomatsu* (KAH•doh•mat•su), or bamboo and pine branches, which are symbols of honesty and consistency.
- Rice cakes, or *mochi* (MO•chee), are offered on a special altar to ancestors and are also eaten for breakfast in a soup called *ozoni* (o•ZO•nee).
- It is considered bad luck to cut *soba* (SO•ba), or buckwheat noodles, when eating them during New Year. For good luck, many children try to eat a whole noodle without chewing it.

Shimenawa

A *shimenawa* (shi•ME•nah•wah) is a rope of braided rice straw decorated with small white paper fans or cloth. It is placed above the entrance of homes to keep evil out of the house during New Year. Have students make shimenawas using raffia. Knot six pieces of raffia (each about 12" in length) at one end. Place a piece of tape across the knot and attach it to a desk or other flat surface. Group the strands into three sections and show the children how to braid the pieces together. Knot the other end to secure the braid. Accordion fold 3" x 3" pieces of white paper to make small fans. Dot glue on the ends of the fans and tuck into the braiding of the shimenawa. Hang all the shimenawas around the door and windows to decorate the classroom in the New Year.

Daruma

A *daruma* (dar•OO•mah) is a wishing doll that is given to someone at the start of a new venture, for example, on a birthday or when celebrating the New Year. A daruma is balanced so that it can not be knocked over, which symbolizes recovery from misfortune. A daruma's eyes are not painted on when the doll is bought. The owner makes a wish as she paints on one eye and if the wish comes true, she paints on the other eye. Let students make their own darumas and make wishes for the New Year. Fill a small round balloon with rice, beans, or sand and blow it up. Each student can place the "doll" on a table, knot end up, and tap it lightly. The doll will stand back up. Decorate the balloon with permanent markers to look like a doll, but do not draw eyes. Then, ask each student to make a New Year wish and draw one eye on her daruma. The other eye can be drawn when her wish comes true!

27

Did You Know?

- In Scotland, New Year is called *Hogmanay* (hog•man•AY). The traditional New Year song, *Auld Lang Syne*, is from Scotland.

- The most famous New Year tradition in Scotland is called *first footing*. The first person to set foot over your threshold on New Year's Day brings you good luck or bad luck. Men, who are considered to be good luck, go from house to house, crossing thresholds, bringing good luck and a small gift, in the past a lump of coal for the fire, but now usually a cake.

- Bonfires are set to burn up the old year. Sometimes a straw figure, representing the old year, is burned in the fire.

New Year Cards

Make first footing greetings to give to friends and relatives. At midnight in Scotland, it is tradition for someone in the house to rush to open the door and let the old year out and the new year in. Have students trace their feet on construction paper and cut out. Provide another piece of construction paper and have students fold the paper in half, like a card. Draw a picture of a door on the outside and write *Good-bye (current year)!* Write *Welcome (upcoming year)* on the foot cutout. Accordion-fold a strip of paper and glue the foot cutout to one end. Glue the other end to the inside of the card, so that when the card is opened, the New Year will "jump" through the door.

Shortbread and Gingerwine

During New Year, Scottish children enjoy eating shortbread and drinking gingerwine, which is nonalcoholic and similar to gingerale. Enjoy shortbread and gingerale with students and sing *Auld Lang Syne* to celebrate the New Year.

Scottish Shortbread Cookies
1 lb. butter
1 cup confectioner's sugar
4 1/2 cups flour

Mix butter and sugar well. Add flour. Mix well. Flour hands and knead dough. Press into a 9" x 13" pan and slice into squares. Prick each cookie with a fork. Bake at 300° for 1 hour. Run a knife through the cut lines while warm. Makes approximately 32 cookies.

Welcome the New Year!

Sing the traditional New Year song, *Auld Lang Syne* which means *for old time's sake.*

Auld Lang Syne
Should auld acquaintance be forgot
And never brought to mind?
Should auld acquaintance be forgot
And days of auld lang syne?

New Year In Russia

Did You Know?

- In Russia, the New Year is celebrated with a winter festival that starts on January 1 and lasts for several days. During the festival, there are many parties with music, dancing, and children playing in the snow.
- Many Russian New Year traditions are similar to Christmas traditions. This is because many years ago, all Christian holidays were outlawed in Russia, so people transferred their Christmas traditions to New Year to disguise their celebration of that Christian holiday. Today in Russia, people can celebrate Christmas and other Christian holidays, but they still celebrate New Year with "Christmas" traditions.
- People exchange gifts around a New Year fir tree, called a *yolochka* (yol•OCH•kah), which is decorated with ornaments and lights.
- Grandfather Frost, a character similar to Santa, and his helper, Snow Girl, ride a *troika* (TROY•kah), which is a sleigh pulled by a team of three horses, to bring gifts to Russian children at New Year.

Russian Nesting Dolls

A traditional gift given to Russian children at New Year is a set of nesting dolls. If possible, share real nesting dolls or show a picture of them to students and ask why they think they are called "nesting" dolls. Students can make their own nesting dolls with plastic foam cups. Gather two each of three different sized plastic foam cups, small (8 oz.), medium (14 oz.), and large (18 oz.), for each student. Cut off the rims of the two smallest cups. Glue or tape the cups together, one on top of the other, placing the edges together. Then, cut the rim off of one of the medium cups and push it inside the other medium cup. Place the large cups on top of each other, rims together. Allow students to decorate the cups as dolls with a variety of materials, such as paint, wiggly eyes, markers, etc. When complete, place the smallest doll in the bottom of the medium doll and cover with the top, then place the medium doll (with the small doll inside) in the bottom of the large doll and cover with the top. Now each student has her own set of nesting dolls!

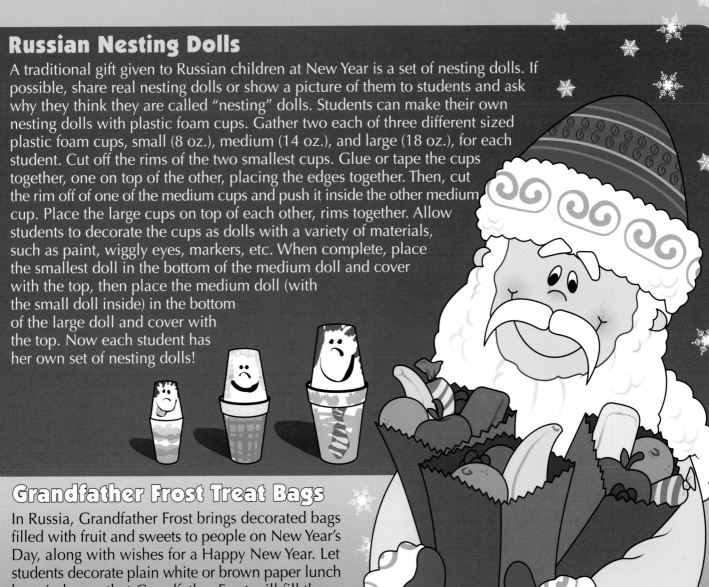

Grandfather Frost Treat Bags

In Russia, Grandfather Frost brings decorated bags filled with fruit and sweets to people on New Year's Day, along with wishes for a Happy New Year. Let students decorate plain white or brown paper lunch bags in hopes that Grandfather Frost will fill them with goodies. Collect the bags and fill them with fruit, such as apples or oranges and sweets like candy or cookies. Add a note from Grandfather Frost, wishing students a Happy New Year. Place the bags on a table and let students find their bags and enjoy the treats!

29

Did You Know?

- Saint Sylvester, a former Pope, is honored on New Year's Eve in Austria, Belgium, Germany, and Switzerland.
- In many areas of Austria, parades are held in which people, called Sylvesterklauses, wear detailed masks and large bells in honor of Saint Sylvester.
- At midnight, church bells ring and trumpets blare. People set off firecrackers, blow horns, and shake noisemakers.
- Church is attended on New Year's Day and a dinner of roast suckling pig is served in the afternoon. Pig is served because pigs cannot walk backward. The hope is that the New Year will progress forward.
- Austrians buy many good luck charms in anticipation of the New Year. These charms include figures of chimney sweeps, pigs with curly tails, four leaf clovers, horseshoes, and mushrooms.

Good Luck Tokens

Every year in Austria, a special New Year token, or *gluecksmuenze* (GLICKS•mint•she), is minted from silver or gold with lucky symbols on one side and New Year's wishes on the other. Give each child a large circle cut from oaktag to make her own New Year token. Draw traditional Austrian good luck symbols, including clovers, mushrooms, pigs, and horseshoes on one side, and write a New Year's message on the back. Paint or color the coin and decorate the edges with silver and gold glitter. If desired, punch a hole in the top and hang with a piece of string.

Lucky Pig

Pigs are considered to be a symbol of good luck in the New Year in Austria. In addition to roast pig for dinner on New Year's Day, people eat pig-shaped candy called *gluecksweinchen* (glick•SHVINE•shen), and buy good luck charms shaped like pigs. Let students create pig cupcakes and enjoy the good luck when eating them. Frost cupcakes with pink frosting and let students place two chocolate candy kisses at the tops for pointed ears, two mini chocolate chips pointed down for eyes, marshmallows in the middle for the snouts with two red cinnamon candies stuck on with frosting for nostrils.

30

New Year In Brazil

Did You Know?

- During New Year in Brazil, towns are decorated with brightly colored streamers and flowers. Fireworks, bells, and sirens ring in the New Year.
- *Feliz Ano Novo* (feh•LEES•AH•no NOH•voh) means *Happy New Year* in Portuguese, the language spoken in Brazil.
- Families celebrate together over a traditional New Year's Eve dinner at midnight that includes lentils, a symbol of wealth for the New Year. A dessert called *rabanada* (rah•bah•NAH•dah), which is similar to French toast, is eaten. After the meal, children go to bed and adults go to parties and elegant balls.

The Queen of the Sea

A beautiful ceremony of African origin is held New Year's Eve on the beaches in Rio de Janeiro in Brazil. People dress in white, place lighted candles in the sand, and wade into the water to throw flowers and gifts to the Queen of the Sea. Have students use their imaginations to write a biography of the Queen of the Sea. Have them tell who she is, what she looks like, where she lives, and what she does. Have each child draw a picture of the Sea Queen and glue it to a piece of construction paper. If desired, have students add sand and draw candles to sprinkle with glitter so they glow. Cut flowers from colorful paper and glue around the picture, creating a frame of flowers. Let each student share his biography. Display the framed pictures on a bulletin board.

Rabanada

Follow the recipe to treat students to a snack that is similar to rabanada.

Ingredients

6 eggs	butter
2 cups milk	cinnamon
12 slices of bread	sugar

Beat the eggs in a large bowl. Add the milk and mix well. Heat a frying pan over medium heat and melt 1 tbsp. butter in the pan. Dip a slice of bread in the egg and milk mixture and place in the hot pan. Cook until golden brown, flip to other side, and cook until brown. Add more butter for each additional piece. Serve warm with a sprinkle of cinnamon and sugar. Serves 12.

New Year In Greece

Saint Basil

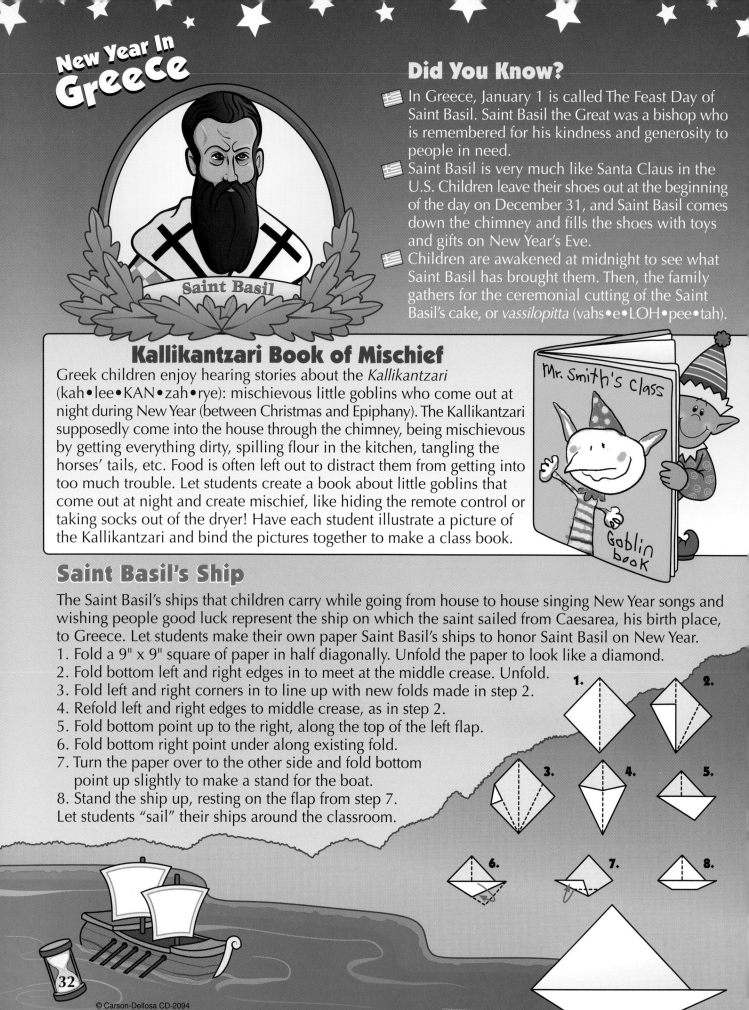

Did You Know?

- In Greece, January 1 is called The Feast Day of Saint Basil. Saint Basil the Great was a bishop who is remembered for his kindness and generosity to people in need.
- Saint Basil is very much like Santa Claus in the U.S. Children leave their shoes out at the beginning of the day on December 31, and Saint Basil comes down the chimney and fills the shoes with toys and gifts on New Year's Eve.
- Children are awakened at midnight to see what Saint Basil has brought them. Then, the family gathers for the ceremonial cutting of the Saint Basil's cake, or *vassilopitta* (vahs•e•LOH•pee•tah).

Kallikantzari Book of Mischief

Greek children enjoy hearing stories about the *Kallikantzari* (kah•lee•KAN•zah•rye): mischievous little goblins who come out at night during New Year (between Christmas and Epiphany). The Kallikantzari supposedly come into the house through the chimney, being mischievous by getting everything dirty, spilling flour in the kitchen, tangling the horses' tails, etc. Food is often left out to distract them from getting into too much trouble. Let students create a book about little goblins that come out at night and create mischief, like hiding the remote control or taking socks out of the dryer! Have each student illustrate a picture of the Kallikantzari and bind the pictures together to make a class book.

Mr. Smith's class

Goblin book

Saint Basil's Ship

The Saint Basil's ships that children carry while going from house to house singing New Year songs and wishing people good luck represent the ship on which the saint sailed from Caesarea, his birth place, to Greece. Let students make their own paper Saint Basil's ships to honor Saint Basil on New Year.

1. Fold a 9" x 9" square of paper in half diagonally. Unfold the paper to look like a diamond.
2. Fold bottom left and right edges in to meet at the middle crease. Unfold.
3. Fold left and right corners in to line up with new folds made in step 2.
4. Refold left and right edges to middle crease, as in step 2.
5. Fold bottom point up to the right, along the top of the left flap.
6. Fold bottom right point under along existing fold.
7. Turn the paper over to the other side and fold bottom point up slightly to make a stand for the boat.
8. Stand the ship up, resting on the flap from step 7.

Let students "sail" their ships around the classroom.

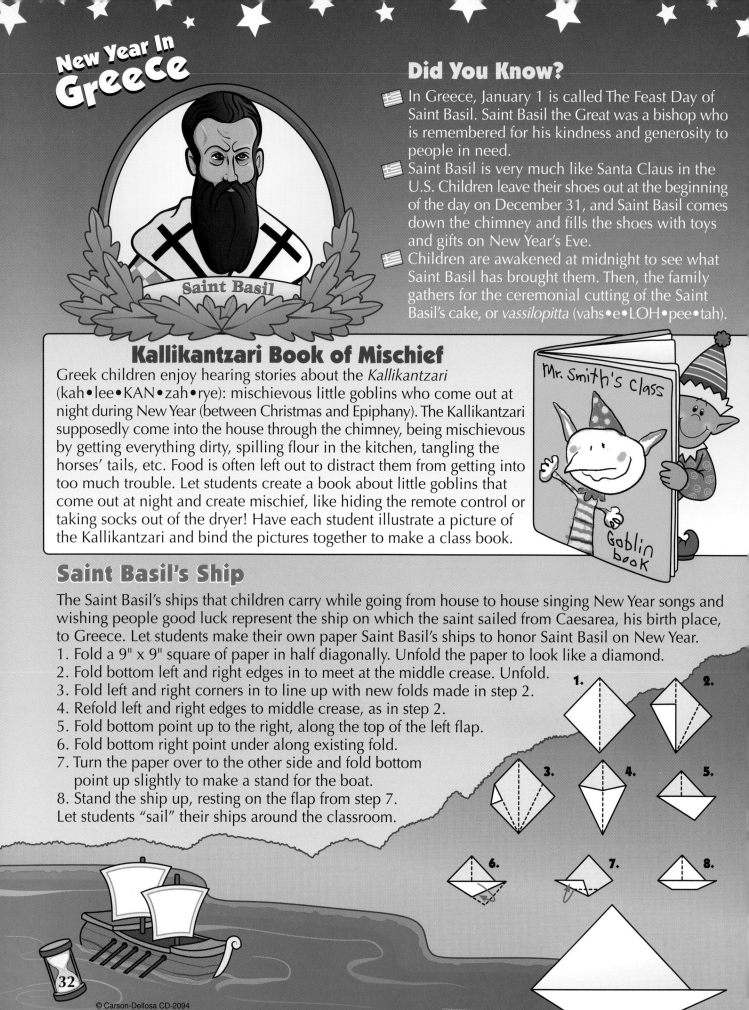

New Year In Iran

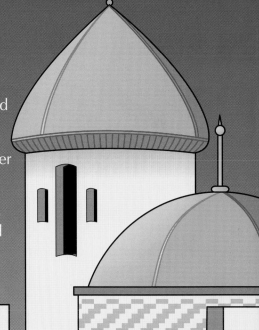

Did You Know?

- In Iran, New Year is celebrated on March 21, the first day of spring.
- The New Year is called *Noruz* (no•ROOZ), which means *new day*.
- Cannon blasts or gunfire signal the start of the new year.
- Iranians visit friends and family, exchange gifts, buy new clothes, and prepare special New Year displays.
- On the last Wednesday before March 21, many families observe the custom of setting small fires in the front yard and having each member of the family jump over the flames for good luck in the new year.
- The 13th and last day of Noruz is called *Sizdah-Bedar* (seez•DAH-bee•DAR), meaning *13th day out*. It is believed that it is bad luck to stay indoors on this day. Iranians stay outside all day picnicking, and leaving all of the bad luck associated with the number 13 outside.

Spring Sprouts

In anticipation for Noruz, the Iranian people sprout grain seed or beans in shallow dishes. These dish gardens are called *sabzeh* (sab•ZEH) and represent new life and growth in the new year. The sabzeh is kept throughout Noruz and is thrown away outdoors on Sizdah-Bedar, symbolizing the throwing away of bad luck. Let students create a sabzeh by sprouting beans in plastic lids. Place several lentil beans in a shallow dish of water. When the skins crack on the beans, peel off and place the lid in a sunny window. Sprouts will take about one week to grow. Throw the sprouts away on the 13th day of the year.

Seven S's

An important part of Noruz is the preparation of the *Haft-Sin*, a special table arranged with seven things that start with "s" (in the Persian language), including a hyacinth plant, the sabzeh (see above activity), wheat pudding, vinegar, sumac herb, an apple, and olives. The items in the Haft-Sin are thought to bring good luck and happiness in the new year. Have students think of seven items that start with "s" in English that they could place in a New Year display. Give each child a piece of brown construction paper to represent a table. Have her look through magazines for pictures of items that start with the letter "s," cut them out, and glue them on her paper table. Display the "tables" on a bulletin board with the title *Lucky S's*.

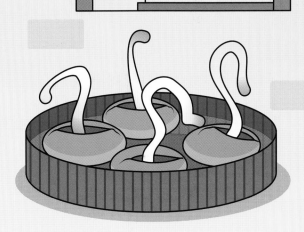

33

Baby New Year

Father Time

lucky money packet

COPY and CUT

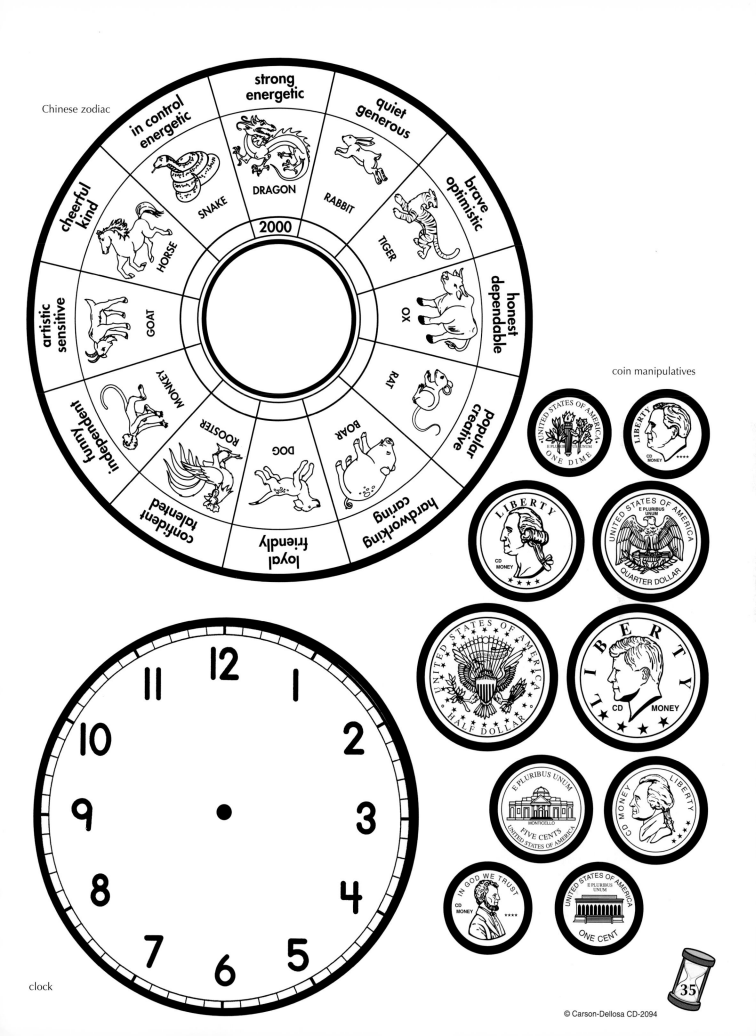

Chinese zodiac

coin manipulatives

clock

35

SOUP'S ON!

Serve up some fun with these soup activites!

Did You Know?

Archaeological evidence suggests the first soup was made with hippopotamus bones!

Literature Selections

Chicken Soup with Rice

by Maurice Sendak: Harper-Collins Children's Books, 1962. (Picture book, 48 pg.) Lively rhyming text celebrates the months of the year and chicken soup.

Famous Seaweed Soup

by Antoinette Truglio Martin: Albert Whitman & Company, 1993. (Picture book, 28 pg.) One day at the beach, Sara makes seaweed soup and declares that anyone who did not help her make her concoction must eat some.

Little Bear

by Else Homelund Minarik: Harper Trophy, 1978. (Picture book, 63 pg.) A tender and eloquent story about Little Bear making his own birthday soup.

Soup Du Jour

These classroom concoctions are sure to be original! Encourage students to think of creative and silly soup combinations, then have them illustrate their interesting creations using the soup kettle pattern (page 38). After a class vote, award a certificate for the most unusual soup creation.

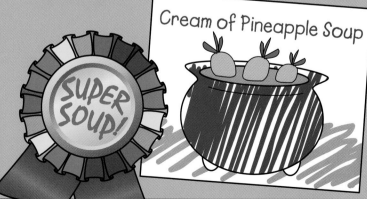

SUPER SOUP!

Cream of Pineapple Soup

Friendship Soup

Serve up a helping of friendship soup with this character education activity. Enlarge the soup kettle pattern (page 38) and post it on a wall or bulletin board. Give each child a copy of a vegetable pattern (page 38) to cut out. Students can write a trait or phrase describing friendship, such as *honesty*, *trustworthiness*, *loyalty*. Make a batch of friendship soup by having children come up one at a time, read their descriptions to the class, and tape their vegetables to the soup kettle.

Check Out the Labels

What is your favorite soup? Let students answer this question by designing soup labels for their choices. Give each child a strip of white paper sized to fit a soup can. Have students illustrate slogans and pictures of their favorite soups or their concoctions from *Soup Du Jour* (page 36) on the paper strips. Ask each student to bring in a soup can and let him wrap and tape his label over the label on the can. Create a graph by grouping and counting similar soups.

Tasty Chicken Noodle Soup

Nothing warms up a cold January day better than a bowl of soup. Prepare chicken noodle soup for your students to enjoy. Makes 8 servings.

Mix all ingredients together in a large saucepan. Bring to a boil, then reduce heat and simmer 10-15 minutes.

Ingredients:
1 large can chunk chicken
3 cans chicken broth
2 cans mixed vegetables
2 cups small egg noodles
salt and pepper to taste

37

onion

celery

COPY and CUT

carrot

potato

soup kettle

38

© Carson-Dellosa CD-2094

100th Day Celebration

Five, four, three, two, one...the 100th day of school is finally here! Mark this happy occasion using the following activities.

Literature Selections

1. The 100th Day of School by Angela Shelf Medearis: Scholastic, Inc., 1996. (Picture book, 32 pg.) A class celebrates the 100th day of school by baking cookies, counting pennies, and making special hats.

2. 100th Day Worries by Margery Cuyler: Simon & Schuster, 2000. (Picture book, 32 pg.) A first grader worries about what to bring to school for the 100th day celebration.

3. Miss Bindergarten Celebrates the 100th Day of Kindergarten by Joseph Slate: Penguin Putnam Books, 1998. (Picture book, 32 pg.) Each student in Miss Bindergarten's class brings in a special project to celebrate the 100th day.

Celebration Crowns

Kick off your 100th day celebration by having children make festive crowns. Give each child a copy of the crown pattern (page 42) to decorate and cut out. Cut 2"-wide strips of poster board or oaktag and size a strip to fit around each student's head. Have children glue the pattern to the headband, then tape or staple the ends of the headband together to make a crown.

Museum of 100

One hundred buttons, 100 beads, 100 marshmallows—all of these items can be found in your class museum of 100. Cover a bulletin board or wall with paper, then use colorful masking tape to divide it into sections. Provide small items such as pennies, cereal, and cotton balls. Pair students and give each a container of items to count into groups of 100. Have students cut 100" lengths of yarn, ribbon, and string as well. Place the objects in resealable plastic bags and label them. Post the bags on the bulletin board with the title *Our 100 Museum*. For an added challenge, give each student a mixed bag of 100 items and have him graph how many of each item is in the bag. Then, add the numbers together to get 100.

Our 100 Museum

100 Words

What is a *centenarian*? A *centennial*? Students can quickly find out using their one hundred dictionaries. Explain that *cent* comes from the Latin word *centum* that means one hundred. *Cent* often appears in words that have one hundred in their meanings. Challenge students to make a booklet of one hundred-related words using a dictionary as reference. Let pairs of students quiz each other using their dictionary words. Have younger students make simple dictionaries that have one hundred words using word wall words, spelling words, etc.

Book of 100 Riddles

Here's a riddle book with a twist! Instead of trying to find the answer to a riddle, have students think of a riddle for the answer. To make a riddle book, cut several sheets of paper into fourths. Cut away the lower right corner on each sheet. Give each child a booklet page and have him write a riddle to which the answer is 100. Finish the booklet by making a back cover out of heavy paper. In the bottom right corner of the back cover, draw a number 100 and glue on glitter. Combine the book pages and add a front cover. Let the children read their riddles to the class.

Count to One Hundred, Then Eat!

Counting leads to snacking when students help make this tasty treat. Bring a variety of snack mix items, such as nuts, raisins, chocolate candies, pretzels and cereal squares. Divide the class into small groups and have each child wash her hands, count out 100 pieces of each snack food, then mix them in large bowls. Enjoy the one hundred snack mix at your classroom celebration.

Picture Perfect

Capture the fun of your celebration with student photographs. Make a large *Happy 100th Day!* sign, complete with festive decorations. Let students wear their *Celebration Crowns* (page 39) and hold the sign while you take pictures. Post the pictures on a 100th Day bulletin board display or let students make and decorate craft stick frames for the pictures as keepsakes.

40

100 Day Olympics

Motivate students to go for the gold in your 100th Day Olympics. Challenge students to do 100 jumping jacks or toe touches. Organize the class into pairs and see who can toss a ball back and forth 100 times without dropping it. Take the class outside and use a stopwatch to see who can run the farthest in 100 seconds. At the conclusion of the games, give each child a copy of the 100th Day Olympics medal pattern (page 42).

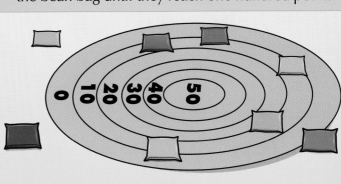

Add It Up to 100

Toss some fun into your 100th Day celebration with a bean bag game. Draw and cut out a 24" circle from poster board. Draw five smaller circles inside the large circle to make a target. Label the outside circle 0, the next 10, the next 20, continuing to the center circle which should be labeled 50. Place the target on the floor and have students stand several feet away. Then, let students take turns tossing a bean bag on the circle and adding up the points they receive. Students keep tossing the bean bag until they reach one hundred points.

Happy 100 Cake

End your celebration on a sweet note with a delicious 100 cake. Begin with two cake mixes. Prepare one cake mix and bake two round cakes. Prepare the second mix and bake one loaf cake, using any remaining batter to make cupcakes. Place the finished cakes on a large foil-covered piece of cardboard and arrange them to resemble the number 100. Decorate the cake with confetti frosting and tube icing. Place cupcakes decorated as balloons around the cake. Let students enjoy the cake as they work on the *Hidden Message* worksheet (page 43).

41

Happy

100th Day of School

I participated in the
100th Day Olympics

100th Day
Olympics
Medal

crown

COPY and CUT

I participated in the
100th Day Olympics

100th Day
Olympics
Medal

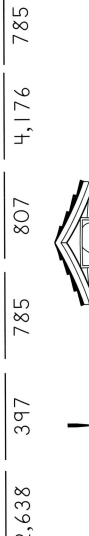
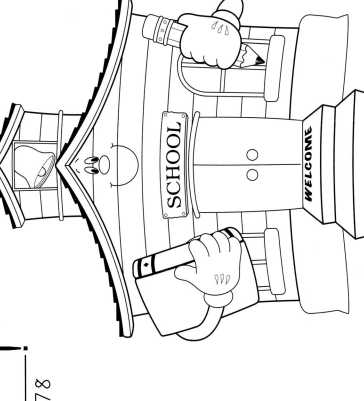

Name _____

Hidden Message

Circle the number in the hundreds place in each number below. Then, use the code to find the missing letters in the puzzle by matching the number in the hundreds place to its letter.

9,901   397   4,176   491   1,037   533   533   785   807   4,176   785

785   1,037   491   2,638   397   785   278

278   !

Code

0 = A   4 = H
3 = N   7 = D
6 = U   2 = Y
9 = O   5 = P
1 = E   8 = R

Louis Braille

French born Louis Braille (January 4, 1809–January 6, 1852) invented the braille system when he was only 15. At age three, he picked up an awl and tried to poke it through leather as he had seen his father do. The awl glanced off the leather and pierced his left eye. The resulting infection spread and he was totally blind by age five. At age ten, at the National Institute for the Young Blind in Paris, he read all 14 of the institute's bulky, raised-print books in his first year. His love of learning and desire to read drove him to experiment with various codes. During vacations, he used an awl to punch holes in leather scraps; at school he used a knitting needle to punch holes in paper. He worked for three years to develop the raised dot system and when complete, his fellow students named it *Braille* in his honor.

Did You Know?

- Before the invention of braille, a typical book had to be divided into twenty volumes, often totalling 400 pounds.

- Millions of people read books, magazines, and newspapers produced by braille printing presses. There are braille greeting cards, wristwatches, and computers; elevators and automated bank machines offer braille directions.

- Braille is the standard form of reading and writing for the blind in virtually every language and can be read at speeds comparable to print.

Literature Selections

Out of Darkness: The Story of Louis Braille by Russell Freedman: Houghton Mifflin Company, 1999. (Biography, 88 pg.) A compelling story of a gifted and generous boy. Includes black and white illustrations, diagrams of braille alphabet, and the slate and stylus used to create it.

The World at His Fingertips: A Story About Louis Braille by Barbara O'Conner: The Lerner Publishing Group, 1997. (Biography, 64 pg.) Presents an inspiring portrait of Braille for children.

Braille: The Boy who Invented Books for the Blind by Margaret Davidson: Scholastic, Inc., 1991. (Biography, 80 pg.) The story of the development of the braille reading system.

Walk a Mile...

Reading in braille involves using the sense of touch in place of eyesight. Help children understand how a blind person uses touch by placing objects, such as crayons or erasers, in a shoebox. Let students use their sense of touch to identify the items with their eyes closed or while blindfolded.

Braille Names

Gain an understanding of how braille is read. Place an enlarged copy of the lowercase braille alphabet (page 45) on a wall. Give each student a copy of the Braille Alphabet Grid (page 45) and have her glue enough boxes for each letter of her first name on a piece of construction paper. Have each student write one letter of her name above each box. Students can write their names by gluing split peas or button candies in each section of the grid to indicate the braille letters.

Braille Alphabet Grid

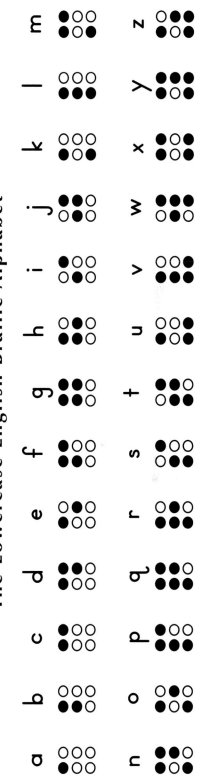

The Lowercase English Braille Alphabet*

a ⠁	b ⠃	c ⠉	d ⠙
e ⠑	f ⠋	g ⠛	h ⠓
i ⠊	j ⠚	k ⠅	l ⠇
m ⠍	n ⠝	o ⠕	p ⠏
q ⠟	r ⠗	s ⠎	t ⠞
u ⠥	v ⠧	w ⠺	x ⠭
y ⠽	z ⠵		

*Each uppercase letter is made by placing an extra dot to the lower left of the lowercase letter.

45

LET IT SNOW!

When the winter snow begins to fall, catch your students' attention with these frosty craft, science, and writing activities.

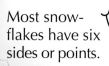

Did You Know?

Most snowflakes have six sides or points.

Snowflakes are made up of tiny ice crystals that stick together as they fall. Snowflakes can contain from 2-200 ice crystals.

Scientist Wilson Bentley developed a technique to photograph snowflakes. He took over 6,000 pictures of individual snowflakes and found that no two were exactly alike.

Literature Selections

The Snowman by Raymond Briggs: Random House, Inc., 1978 (Picture book, 32 pg.) This wordless picture book tells the story of a boy who builds a snowman that comes to life.

Snip, Snip...Snow! by Nancy Poydar: Holiday House, 1997 (Picture book, 30 pg.) While waiting for a big snowstorm, Sophie finds a way to make her own snowflakes.

Snowflake Bentley by Jacqueline Briggs Martin: Houghton Mifflin Co., 1998. (Picture book, 32 pg.) Presents the life and work of Wilson Bentley, who studied and photographed snowflakes.

Stopping by Woods on a Snowy Evening by Robert Frost: E.P. Dayton, 1985. (Picture book, 32 pg.) Beautifully detailed illustrations accompany the classic Robert Frost poem.

Snow, Snow by Jane Yolen: Wordsong/Boyds Mills Press, 1998 (Poetry, 32 pg.) Stunning wintertime photographs are accompanied by poems describing the sights and sounds of winter.

It's Snowing, It's Snowing! by Jack Prelutsky: HarperCollins Children's Books, 1985. (Poetry, 48 pg.) The wonders of wintertime are captured in a collection of poems.

Grandmother Winter by Phyllis Root: Houghton Mifflin Co., 1999. (Picture book, 32 pg.) When Grandmother Winter shakes out her goose feather quilt, people and animals prepare for cold and snowy weather.

Let's Build a Snowman!

Build a snowman even when it's not snowing outside! To make an indoor snowman, have students stuff two large, white trash bags with crumpled sheets of newspaper and tie the bags closed. Use heavy-duty clear tape to attach the bags together. Cut out eyes, a nose, and a mouth from construction paper and tape them to the bag. Place a hat on the snowman's head and a scarf around his neck. When your snowman is complete, treat students to hot cocoa and share a picture book from *Literature Selections* (above) with the class.

On a chilly
Winter day,
A snowman is
A cheery sight
He always looks
So nice,
With his top hat
And big smile.

Ode to a Snowman

Talking about snowy weather and snowmen is sure to inspire young writers! Have students write poems about winter weather or snowmen, then display them with snowman pictures. Begin by giving each student a half-sheet of 9" x 12" construction paper. Then, instruct each student to make a snowman by tearing three circles from white paper. Have him glue the circles to resemble a snowman on the left side of the paper. Decorate the snowman using buttons, twigs, and construction paper. On the right side, have each student write her poem.

Frosty Snowman Cupcakes

These frosty cupcakes will warm up a cold winter's day! Bake 12 regular-sized cupcakes according to package directions and using cupcake liners. Then, bake 12 miniature cupcakes without liners. Frost the cupcakes using vanilla icing. Center a small cupcake on top of each regular cupcake to create a snowman. Sprinkle the snowman with shredded coconut. Use chocolate chips and candy buttons to decorate the snowman. Make a scarf by tying lengths of ribbon or licorice strips around the bottom of the small cupcake. Share the cupcakes with the class.

Stuffed Snowman

These plump snowmen will add a festive touch to your wintertime classroom décor. Have each child trace two copies of the snowman pattern (page 54) on white paper. Put the patterns together, leaving the top open. Use markers, buttons, and yarn to decorate the snowman. Then, stuff the snowman with cotton balls, and glue the two patterns together at the top. Make a scarf using a twisted pipe cleaner. Display the completed snowmen on a bulletin board or hang them from the ceiling.

47

How to Build a Snowman

These step-by-step directions will make building a snowman easier than ever! Give each student three paper plates. Connect the plates by punching a hole in the bottom of one, at the top and bottom of the second, and in the top of the third. Loop short pieces of pipe cleaner through the holes in the first and second plates and the second and third plates and twist the ends together in the back. After the plates are connected, provide sunflower seeds, construction paper, felt, and brown pipe cleaners for decorating the snowmen. Instruct students to write the steps to building a snowman on the bottom two plates, starting at the bottom. Write the last step on a construction paper hat, then attach the hat to the snowman.

Finally, put a hat on the snowman's head.

Roll a small snowball for the snowman's head. Make a face and put a scarf around his neck.

Add arms and buttons.

Roll a smaller snowball to put on top of the larger one.

Roll a large snowball for the bottom of the snowman.

Cute as a Button Snowman

With a few buttons and a little creativity, students can make adorable snowman necklaces. Give each student three large, white two-hole buttons. Stack the buttons, turning the top button sideways, so the button holes resemble eyes. Turn the two bottom buttons upright so the button holes resemble the buttons on a snowman. Glue the bottom of one button to the top of the one below it. Allow the glue to dry completely. Provide pieces of construction paper, felt, and ribbon to use to make hats and scarves for the snowmen. To make a necklace, thread a piece of thin, plastic filament through the two top button holes (snowman eyes) and knot the ends.

Snow-Free Snowmen

These soapy snowmen are a snow-free version of the real thing. To make approximately four snowmen, mix 4 cups of soap flakes (such as Ivory Snow®) and 1/2 cup of water in a large bowl. Blend with an electric mixer until the ingredients reach a doughy consistency. Give each child a portion of the dough and instruct her to roll one large ball and two slightly smaller balls. Stack the balls on top of each other with the largest on the bottom. Use toothpicks to hold the balls together. Small twigs can be used to make arms. Push small colorful beads into the dough to create eyes, mouth, and buttons. Use markers to color a toothpick piece orange for the snowman's nose. Allow the dough to dry for several hours.

48

Snowflake Shape Poems

Children can write poetry as delicate as snowflakes. Give each child an enlarged copy of the snowflake pattern (page 54) and have her cut it out. Have each student compose a poem about snow, then write the poem around the pattern, so the poem takes the shape of the snowflake. Let students cut around their poems to create snowflake designs. Glue the snowflakes to construction paper and display them on a bulletin board.

Snowflake Poem

Snow falling white and fluffy on the ground. See the snowmen with their big smiles and tall hats. The snow swirls, twirls, and cascades through the sky. The air is crisp and cold and the snow crunches under my red boots.

By Shawn

Pretty Pasta Snowflakes

Bow tie, wagon wheel, macaroni—these are just some types of pasta students can use to make unique snowflakes. Give each student a piece of waxed paper and provide a variety of pasta for students to use to create designs. Instruct students to glue their completed designs together with white glue. When the glue has dried, carefully peel the snowflakes off the waxed paper. If desired, use hot glue to attach a length of fishing line to the top of the snowflake to create a hanger.

Here Comes the Snow!

Children can make snowflake designs as individual and unique as actual snowflakes. Give each child a white paper circle and instruct her to fold it in half, then in thirds, then in half again. Have students cut designs around the outer edges. Unfold the paper to see the snowflake. To make the snowflakes sparkle, spread a thin layer of glue on the snowflakes, then sprinkle clear glitter over them. Glue the snowflakes to circles of construction paper.

① ② ③ ④ ⑤

49

Catch Some Snowflakes!

The next time the snow falls, take your class on a wintry snowflake hunt! Give each child a small piece of black construction paper or black velvet. Place the paper or fabric in a freezer for several hours until frozen. During a snowfall, have students hold up the paper or fabric pieces to catch the snowflakes as they fall. Use a magnifying glass to look at the snowflakes before they melt. Encourage children to describe or draw the snowflakes they find.

Sparkling Snowflakes

Create snowflakes that will "stick around" through the winter. To make a self-sticking snowflake, choose a snowflake pattern (page 55). Place the snowflake pattern in a resealable plastic bag. Use white glue to trace the snowflake onto the plastic bag. Sprinkle clear glitter over the wet glue. Allow the snowflake to dry for several days. When the glue is dry, carefully peel the snowflake off the plastic and adhere to room-temperature classroom windows for a wintry sight. Use clear tape to adhere the snowflakes to cold windows.

Snowy Scenes

Have students cover their winter pictures with freshly fallen snow using snow paint. Have students draw and color snowy day scenes on dark blue construction paper. Then, use the recipe below to make snow paint to accent the pictures.

Snow Paint

1/2 cup flour	1/2 cup water
1/2 cup salt	Clean squeeze bottle

Mix the ingredients together and spoon the mixture into a squeeze bottle. (An empty glue bottle works well.) Squeeze the mixture onto construction paper. The paint will dry 3-dimensional and white. The recipe makes enough paint to fill a $7^5/_8$-ounce glue bottle.

50

Crystal Snowflakes

Capture the beauty of snowflakes indoors.

1. Cut a white pipe cleaner into three equal sections.
2. Twist the pipe cleaner pieces together in the center to create a snowflake shape. Trim the ends so all are even.
3. Tie string around the outer edges to make a snowflake shape. Tie string to the top of one pipe cleaner and tie the opposite end of the string to the center of a pencil.
4. Fill a large wide-mouth jar with one cup of boiling water. Mix three tablespoons of 20 Mule Team Borax Laundry Booster® soap, one at a time, into the water. Stir until the soap is dissolved (some powder may settle on the bottom).
5. Suspend the pipe cleaner snowflake in the water by resting the pencil across the top of the jar. Leave the snowflake in the mixture overnight. The next day, the snowflake should be covered with shimmering crystals! If desired, send the directions for this activity home so parents and children can make their own sparkling crystal snowflakes.

Laundry Booster

The Sweetest Snowflake

What's white, fluffy, and sweet? Marshmallow snowflakes! Use miniature marshmallows and toothpicks to make 3-dimensional snowflakes. Begin by pushing six toothpicks into a miniature marshmallow. Then, put marshmallows on the ends of each toothpick and continue adding toothpicks and marshmallows to form a snowflake shape.

One, Two, Three, Freeze!

How long does it take water to turn into ice? Find out with this activity. Fill two plastic containers (margarine tubs work well) with water. Put one container in the freezer and leave the other at room temperature. Have students measure the temperature every half hour. How cold does the water get in each container? How many degrees does the temperature change? Record the results in a class journal.

Make Your Own Icicle

With some patience and a little luck, your class can make an icicle. Find a large container with a handle. Puncture a small hole in the bottom of the container, large enough to allow water to drip out slowly. Fill the container with water and hang it outside during days and nights when the temperature will be at or near freezing. After several days, the freezing, thawing, and refreezing of the dripping water will form an icicle on the bottom of the container. If an icicle does not form after a few days, move the container to another location or change the size of the hole at the bottom.

Paint the Snow

Let your class add a touch of color to the snow outside. Fill several spray bottles with water and add several drops of food coloring. Tightly place the tops on the spray bottles. Shake each bottle to mix the water and food coloring together. Take the bottles outside and let the children decorate the snow-covered ground or snow drifts by spraying the mixture on the snow.

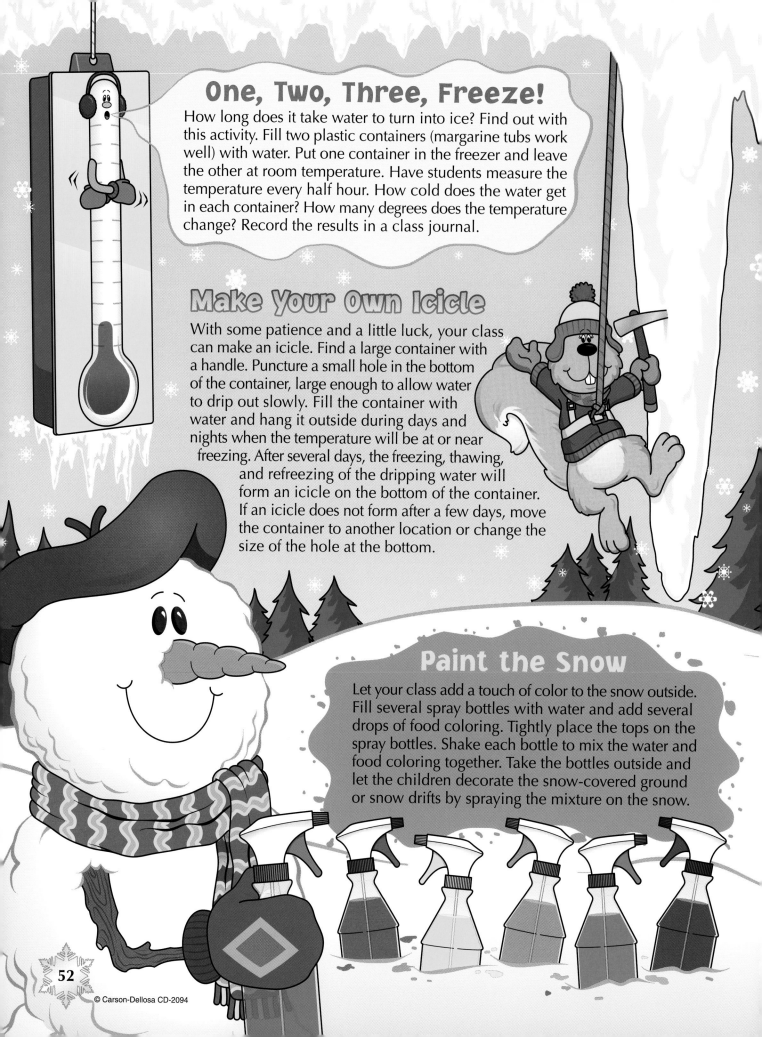

52

Winter Mitten Wreath

Warm up cold, wintry days with a cozy classroom mitten wreath. Give each student a sheet of construction paper and have him cut out and decorate a mitten shape. Let students glue their mittens around a large ring cut from poster board. Make a hanger for the finished wreath using colorful yarn. Hang the wreath in the classroom.

Snow Globes

Capture the quiet beauty of a snowy day with snow globes. Give each child a large circle of blue paper. Have him draw and color a wintertime scene on the circle. Give each student a piece of clear plastic wrap. Turn the circle over and center it on the plastic wrap. Have students cut the plastic wrap into a circle shape that is slightly larger than the paper circle. Fold and tape the edges of the plastic wrap to the back of the circle, leaving a small opening. Pour some clear glitter through the opening; then tape it closed. Let each student cut out a snow globe base from brown paper and tape it to the back. When students shake their snow globes, sparkling snow will fall across their winter scenes.

Glitter

Bundling up Booklets

What do you wear in the snow? Let students illustrate their answers with these snowy day booklets. Give each student several sheets of paper. Provide fabric, felt, wallpaper, and construction paper pieces for children to use to cut out hats, mittens, boots, scarves, and coats. Each student can glue one piece of winter clothing on each page, write a description, and tell how she gets ready to play outside on a snowy day. Staple the booklets together and have students read them aloud to their classmates. Place the completed booklets at a reading center for students to enjoy during free time.

When I want to play in the snow

Sam T.

I put on my coat.

I put on my scarf.

snowflake

COPY and CUT

snowman

POLAR ANIMALS

Take students on an icy tour of the Arctic and Antarctic! Along the way, they will learn about the North and South Poles and the animals that call these frozen places home.

DID YOU KNOW?

- The Arctic and Antarctica are actually frozen deserts, since very little precipitation falls in either area.
- Just as in hot deserts, mirages occur at both the North and South Poles. They happen when sunlight passes through layers of cold air.
- Fossils found on Antarctica suggest that millions of years ago, the continent was located near the equator and had a much warmer climate.
- The polar bear, orca, Arctic fox, and reindeer live in the Arctic. The penguin and orca live in the Antarctic.

LITERATURE SELECTIONS

Little Penguin by Patrick Benson: Philomel Books, 1990. (Picture book, 40 pg.) Pit the Adélie penguin meets up with a giant whale in the Antarctic.

Ice Bear and Little Fox by Jonathan London: Dutton Children's Books, 1998 (Picture book, 40 pg.) Describes the relationship between a polar bear and an Arctic fox and how they rely on each other for survival.

A Caribou Journey by Debbie S. Miller: Little, Brown, and Company, 1994 (Picture book, 32 pg.) A baby caribou follows her herd as they migrate through the Arctic searching for food.

White Bear, Ice Bear by Michael Rothman: Morrow Junior Books, 1989. (Picture book, 32 pg.) A boy transforms into a polar bear and wanders the Arctic tundra.

Little Penguin's Tale by Audrey Wood: Harcourt Brace Jovanovich, 1989. (Picture book, 40 pg.) Nanny Penguin tells a tale about a mischievous little penguin to her grandchildren.

Little Walrus Warning by Carol Young: Soundprints, 1996. (Picture book, 32 pg.) A walrus prepares her calf to leave the nursery.

ARCTIC AND ANTARCTIC ADAPTATIONS

To survive the extremely cold conditions of the Arctic and Antarctic, animals have special adaptations such as thick fur and layers of blubber under their skin. Some have darker fur that turns white during the winter to camouflage them in the snowy environment. Have children compare how the Arctic polar bear and fox and the Antarctic penguin adapt by making a large class chart. Copy the polar bear, Arctic fox, and emperor penguin patterns (pages 62-64). Divide a large piece of butcher paper into three columns and glue a pattern to the top of each column. Under each animal, have the children write about its adaptations.

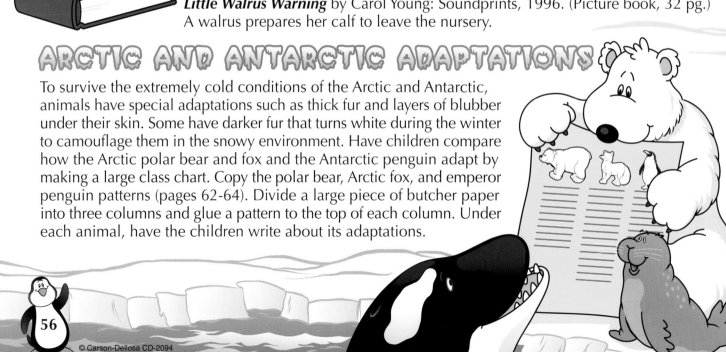

ICY WORDS

In the Arctic and Antarctic, where ice and snow are everywhere, it is not surprising that there are many words for these conditions. Since sea ice is always changing, there are many terms to describe it. Post the ice words below on the chalkboard without definitions. Have each child choose a term and write a description of what the sea ice looks like. Allow children to read their descriptions, then compare them to the definitions.

Candle ice–Thin ice that forms around the shoreline; it twinkles in the sunlight and makes a tinkling sound as it melts

Pancake ice–Small pancake-sized circles of broken ice that float on the water's surface

Ice field–A huge area of flat, frozen ice

Ice floes–Large pieces of floating ice that provide resting areas for animals such as Arctic walruses and Antarctic penguins

CREATE A TUNDRA

The Arctic tundra is a large area within the Arctic Circle that has no trees and little plant life. Create an environment similar to the tundra by filling a large plastic freezer container ³/₄ full of water and freezing it. Tell students that a layer of permanently frozen underground ice (permafrost) in the Arctic Circle does not allow trees and other plants with longer roots to grow. Let students know that the ice from the freezer represents permafrost. Place a layer of soil on top of the ice and freeze overnight. Remove the container from the freezer and have students examine the frozen soil. Allow the soil to thaw and have students observe periodically how the soil on top becomes wet and soggy. Point out that during the Arctic spring, shallow-rooted plants bloom for a short time and the ice above the ground begins to melt. The water on the ground cannot drain through the permafrost so the soil becomes soggy and wet.

BRIGHT POLAR SKIES

The northern lights, or *aurora borealis*, occur in the Arctic skies. The southern dawn, or *aurora australis*, is a similar phenomena that occurs in the Antarctic sky. During these displays, the skies over the North and South Poles are filled with streaks of blue, purple, and green light. Have students use dark blue paper and watercolor paints to create pictures of the northern lights or southern dawn. Color a polar landscape scene on the bottom of the paper. Then, paint streaks across the top of the paper resembling the polar lights. Explain to students as they are painting their pictures that these lights are caused by explosions on the sun's surface. Electric particles fill the atmosphere and are attracted to the magnetic poles.

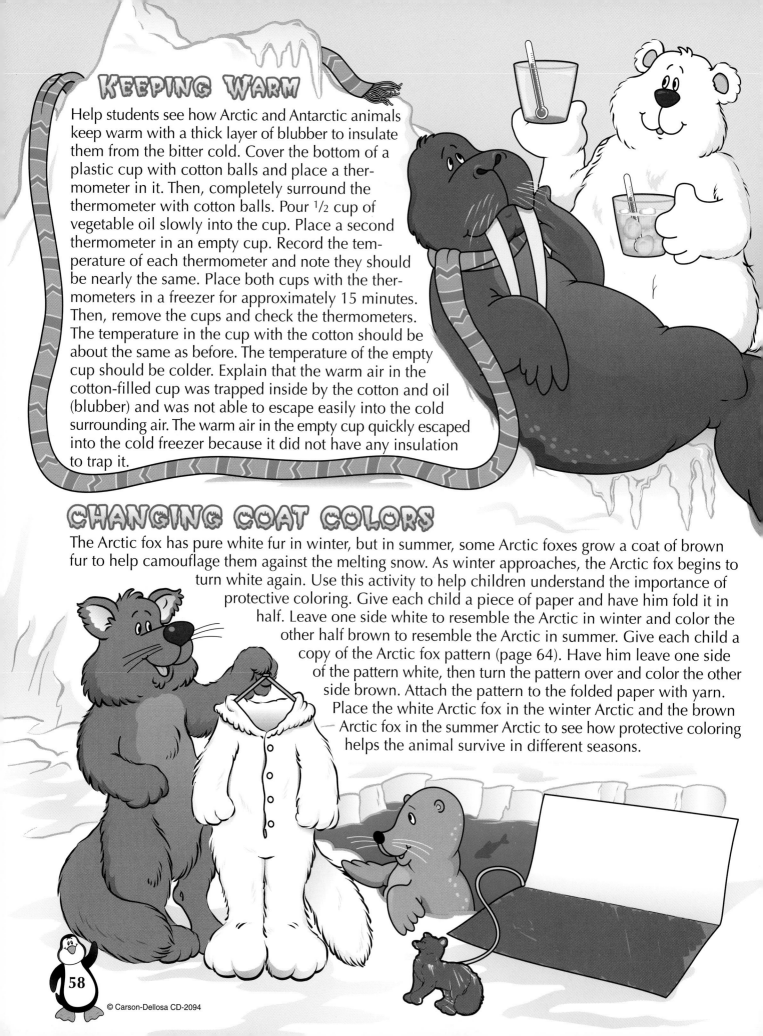

KEEPING WARM

Help students see how Arctic and Antarctic animals keep warm with a thick layer of blubber to insulate them from the bitter cold. Cover the bottom of a plastic cup with cotton balls and place a thermometer in it. Then, completely surround the thermometer with cotton balls. Pour $\frac{1}{2}$ cup of vegetable oil slowly into the cup. Place a second thermometer in an empty cup. Record the temperature of each thermometer and note they should be nearly the same. Place both cups with the thermometers in a freezer for approximately 15 minutes. Then, remove the cups and check the thermometers. The temperature in the cup with the cotton should be about the same as before. The temperature of the empty cup should be colder. Explain that the warm air in the cotton-filled cup was trapped inside by the cotton and oil (blubber) and was not able to escape easily into the cold surrounding air. The warm air in the empty cup quickly escaped into the cold freezer because it did not have any insulation to trap it.

CHANGING COAT COLORS

The Arctic fox has pure white fur in winter, but in summer, some Arctic foxes grow a coat of brown fur to help camouflage them against the melting snow. As winter approaches, the Arctic fox begins to turn white again. Use this activity to help children understand the importance of protective coloring. Give each child a piece of paper and have him fold it in half. Leave one side white to resemble the Arctic in winter and color the other half brown to resemble the Arctic in summer. Give each child a copy of the Arctic fox pattern (page 64). Have him leave one side of the pattern white, then turn the pattern over and color the other side brown. Attach the pattern to the folded paper with yarn. Place the white Arctic fox in the winter Arctic and the brown Arctic fox in the summer Arctic to see how protective coloring helps the animal survive in different seasons.

A BEAR WHITE AS SNOW

Unlike the black bear or grizzly bear, polar bears are entirely white except for their black noses, eyes, and claws. Their coats contain long hollow hairs, called *guard hairs*, that are transparent and allow sunlight to pass through and warm the bear's black skin. Have children make polar bears using the polar bear pattern (page 62). Let each students trace the pattern on black paper using white chalk, then cut out the pattern. Provide white paint and have students paint the polar bears, leaving the noses, eyes, and claws black. Post the polar bears on a white piece of butcher paper to represent their snowy habitat.

POLAR PAWS

The Arctic polar bear is one of the largest and strongest animals in the world. Its huge paws support its weight and act as snowshoes so the bear can easily walk across the snow. An average polar bear paw measures 12" wide and 18" long and has five claws. Help students understand how large a polar bear paw is by having them cut out actual-sized paws from paper. On large sheets of white paper, have students use rulers to measure and mark a line that is 18" tall and another that is 12" wide. Have them draw and cut out a paw shape around the lines, adding paw pads and gluing black paper claws to the top. Have students guess how many of their hands could fit inside the polar bear paws, then find the actual number.

POLAR SHOES

POLAR SHOES
XXXXL
22E

FROZEN OCEANS

The waters of the Arctic and Antarctic Oceans are saltier than in other oceans. Demonstrate how salt water is created in these oceans. Fill two plastic cups each with $\frac{1}{2}$ cup of warm water. Dissolve one teaspoon of salt in each cup. Place cup 1 in a freezer for 1-2 hours or until the top is frozen. Then, lift the ice out of the cup and let students see the small amount of water remaining under the ice. Pour out water from cup 2 until it contains the same amount of water as cup 1. Let both cups sit overnight. The next day, because some water has evaporated from both cups, more salt should be clinging to the sides of cup 1 than cup 2. As you conclude the experiment, explain that when the water in the Arctic and Antarctic Oceans begins to freeze, like in cup 1, the salt drains below the ice, making a layer of cold, extremely salty water, or *brine*, that is directly underneath the ice.

59

REINDEER ANTLERS

Reindeer, or caribou, are a type of deer with large hooves and antlers. Both male and female reindeer have a large, broad antler above their heads called a *shovel* that is used to dig in the snow when searching for food. Have students make reindeer pictures, complete with shovels. Give each child pieces of brown and white paper and have her draw a reindeer face on the white paper. On the brown paper, have her trace one hand three times and the other hand two times and cut out the hand shapes. Glue two hand shapes above the reindeer head, bending the shapes forward slightly. Then, glue the remaining hand shapes to the top of the reindeer head and fold the front hand shape forward. Use these 3-dimensional pictures to help students see how reindeer use their shovel antlers to dig. Tell students that herds of reindeer migrate throughout the Arctic tundra in search of lichen, a type of moss that can take years to grow back.

AN ORCA POD

Orcas live in all the world's oceans, but are most common in the ice packs of the Arctic and Antarctic. Orcas are black except for white markings above their eyes, on their bellies, and under their tail flukes and heads. Recreate the distinct markings of the orca using mosaic. Copy the orca pattern (page 62) on white paper and give one to each student to cut out. Let each student tear black paper into small pieces and glue the paper pieces to the top portion of the pattern, leaving the spaces above the eye and on the underside white. Display the pod of orcas on a bulletin board or wall.

DIVING PENGUINS

Penguins are one of the few animals that live in the bitterly cold Antarctic. Although they cannot fly, penguins have short flippers used for swimming. Solid bones in a penguin's body help them dive deep underwater. Use this experiment to demonstrate how, unlike other birds, penguins are able to dive and find fish to eat. Fill a deep container 3/4 full of water. Place an empty coffee can on the surface and allow it to float open end up. Point out how the can floats high on the water. Float a second can on the surface, but fill it with sand until it sinks a bit. Then, have a student push down the top of both cans at the same time. Point out that the sand-filled can is easier to push down into the water, demonstrating how heavy bones help penguins dive underwater.

SWIMMING PENGUINS

Birds need large wingspans to fly, but would large wings help a penguin swim? Use this experiment to help students understand how short flippers enable penguins to swim better. Fill a large plastic dishpan with water. Cut one short, wide wing shape (about 5" x 3" wide) from poster board to resemble a penguin wing. Cut a long, thin wing (about 8" x 2" wide) from poster board to resemble the wing of a flying bird. Hold the edge of the short wing and push it through the water. Then, hold the edge of the long wing and push it through the water. Point out that the smaller, wider wing moved through the water easier than the longer, thinner wing, demonstrating that a penguin's shorter, stiffer wings are better for swimming.

PAPER PENGUINS

Students can create cute, comical penguins from paper plates. Give each student pieces of black and orange construction paper. Have him use yellow or white crayons to draw a large circle and two teardrop-shaped wings on the black paper, then cut them out. Glue the circle to the top of the plate for the penguin's head and glue the wings on each side. Students can cut out and glue orange triangle shapes to make feet and a beak. Finish the penguins by making eyes with white paper circles and black crayons.

ALL ABOUT POLAR ANIMALS

Help students become experts and share all they have learned about polar animals. Enlarge the polar bear, reindeer, penguin, walrus, arctic fox, and orca patterns (pages 62-64). Divide students into groups and give each group a pattern. Provide reference materials and let students research facts about their polar animals, such as how the animal gets food, how it takes care of its young, and where it lives. Write the facts on the enlarged patterns. Have students color the patterns to resemble the animals, then glue the patterns to a large sheet of paper to make a facts sheet.

61

orca

polar bear

COPY and CUT

COPY and CUT

Emperor penguin

reindeer

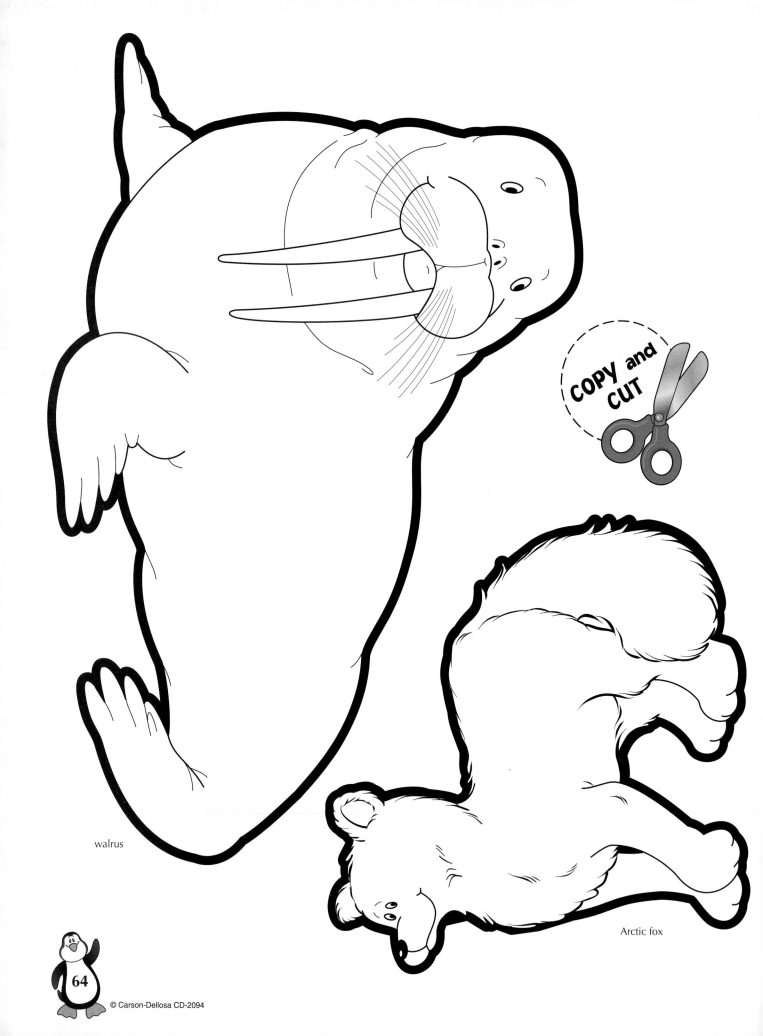

walrus

COPY and CUT

Arctic fox

HONORING DR. MARTIN LUTHER KING, JR.

Dr. Martin Luther King, Jr. is one of the world's best-known advocates for justice and equal rights. Born on January 15, 1929, Dr. King was a leader of the Civil Rights Movement of the 1960's that called for working out conflicts with kindness and love, rather than hatred and violence. Martin Luther King, Jr. continued the fight for equal rights until he was shot and killed in 1968. In the United States, he is remembered and honored with a national holiday on the third Monday of January, which is close to his birthday.

DID YOU KNOW?

- **January 15, 1929**–Martin Luther King, Jr. was born in Atlanta, Georgia.
- **Fall 1944**–King entered Morehouse College at 15, after skipping several grades in high school.
- **Spring 1951**–King graduated from Crozer Theological Seminary and became a minister like his father.
- **June 18, 1953**–King married Coretta Scott in Marion, Alabama.
- **June 1955**–King received a Ph.D. in theology from Boston University in Massachusetts.
- **December 5, 1955**–King led the Montgomery, Alabama bus boycott, sparked by Rosa Parks' refusal to give up her seat on the bus to a white person, as was the law at the time.

- **August 28, 1963**–King delivered his *I Have a Dream* speech to 250,000 spectators in Washington, D.C.
- **1963**–King was named *Time* magazine's Man of the Year.
- **December 1964**–King was awarded the Nobel Peace Prize in Norway. He was the youngest man to win this prize.
- **March 1965**–King led "freedom marchers" for voting rights from Selma, Alabama to Montgomery, Alabama.
- **April 4, 1968**–King was assassinated in Memphis, Tennessee.
- **November 1983**–President Ronald Reagan signed a bill declaring Martin Luther King, Jr.'s birthday a federal holiday.

65

LITERATURE SELECTIONS

My Dream of Martin Luther King by Faith Ringgold: Crown Publishing Group, Inc., 1995. (Picture book, 32 pg.) Describes a dream about the great civil rights leader.

Happy Birthday, Martin Luther King by Jean Marzollo: Scholastic, Inc., 1993 (Picture book, 32 pg.) An easy to understand biography about Martin Luther King, Jr.

A Picture Book of Martin Luther King by David Adler: Holiday House, 1989 (Picture book, 32 pg.) An introduction to the life of Martin Luther King, Jr.

I HAVE A DREAM

On August 28, 1963, Martin Luther King, Jr. delivered his famous *I Have a Dream* speech at the Lincoln Memorial in Washington, D.C. This speech stirred feelings of brotherhood in people across the United States. Help students experience the power of this speech by performing a dramatic reading. Assign each child a section to read or memorize. Let the entire class chime in when the phrases, "I have a dream," and "let freedom ring" are spoken. Read the speech in its entirety first, discussing the meaning and feeling. Then, practice the dramatic reading as a class to coordinate the parts. Perform the reading on or before Martin Luther King, Jr. Day for another class, the entire school, or for parents.

THE CONTENT OF YOUR CHARACTER

In his *I Have a Dream* speech, Dr. King said, "I have a dream that my four children will one day live in a nation where they will not be judged by the color of their skin, but by the content of their character." Ask students if they know what Dr. King meant. Then, brainstorm words that describe how people look and how people act. Have students think about which list of traits is more important. Let each student fold a sheet of paper in half and trace the child pattern (page 69) so the top of the head touches the fold. Cut out the traced figure, making sure not to cut the fold at the head. Let each child decorate the front to look like himself, then unfold and on the inside describe how he acts. Display the completed projects on a wall titled *To Really See Us, Look Inside!*

LET FREEDOM RING

Martin Luther King, Jr. often quoted lines from patriotic and spiritual songs including, "Free at last! Free at last! Thank God Almighty, we are free at last!" from an old African-American spiritual and "Let freedom ring!" from the patriotic song *My Country 'Tis of Thee*. Dr. King knew that all Americans, regardless of skin color, should enjoy the freedom that these songs promise. Talk about what freedoms were denied African-Americans in Dr. King's day. Let each child cut out two bell patterns (page 69), one on yellow paper and one on white paper. Attach the tops of the bells, yellow on top, with a paper fastener. Write *Let Freedom Ring!* on the yellow bell, then have students write about what freedom means to them on the white patterns. Tie yarn to to the paper fastener for hanging.

66

WE SHALL OVERCOME

Dr. King encouraged people not to give up in their struggles for equal rights and fair treatment. To motivate people to persevere, he often used the phrase, "We shall overcome." This phrase comes from an old hymn, which became the unofficial theme song of the Civil Rights Movement. Ask students to think of a time they persevered to achieve a goal. Have them write speeches using personal stories to encourage others. Have students think of motivational phrases, like "keep up the hard work" or "never give up" to repeat in their speeches. Let each student deliver his speech to the class as a motivational boost!

A LIFE OF ACHIEVEMENT

Although Martin Luther King, Jr.'s life was cut short, he achieved more than many people do in a full lifetime. Share Dr. King's accomplishments with students by completing Dr. King's lifetime booklet (page 68). Let students cut out the booklet pages, then color and order them according to the dates on each page. Cut front and back covers from construction paper and staple the pages together. Let students take the booklets home to share with their families.

A PEACEFUL SOLUTION

Dr. King was an advocate for resolving conflicts peacefully. He learned about this "nonviolent resistance" by reading about an Indian leader named Mahatma Gandhi. Gandhi led a revolution in India against the ruling English government without using guns or violence. Encourage students to think of ways to peacefully resolve conflicts in their everyday lives. Have students brainstorm possible conflicts at home, school, during extra-curricular activities, etc. Display several conflicts, such as *another child takes your dessert at lunch every day*. Then, provide copies of the dove pattern (page 69) and challenge students to write peaceful solutions on the doves. Display the doves around each conflict on a wall or bulletin board.

PRIZE FOR PEACE

In 1964, Martin Luther King, Jr. won the Nobel Peace Prize. Based on what they have learned, have students write paragraphs telling why they think King was awarded this prize. Then, have each child glue two red crepe paper streamers to a sheet of white paper from the top corners to the bottom center, forming a V. Glue a yellow paper circle over the bottom point of the V to create a medal. Have each student decorate the medal and write the final copy of her paragraph inside the V. Display the medals with the title *And the Prize Goes To... Martin Luther King, Jr.!*

67

1929: Martin Luther King, Jr. was born.

1951: Dr. King graduates from Seminary and becomes a minister.

1955: Dr. King leads bus boycott in Alabama.

1963: Dr. King delivers his *I Have a Dream* speech.

1964: Dr. King receives the Nobel Peace Prize.

1983: President Reagan declares Martin Luther King, Jr. Day a national holiday.

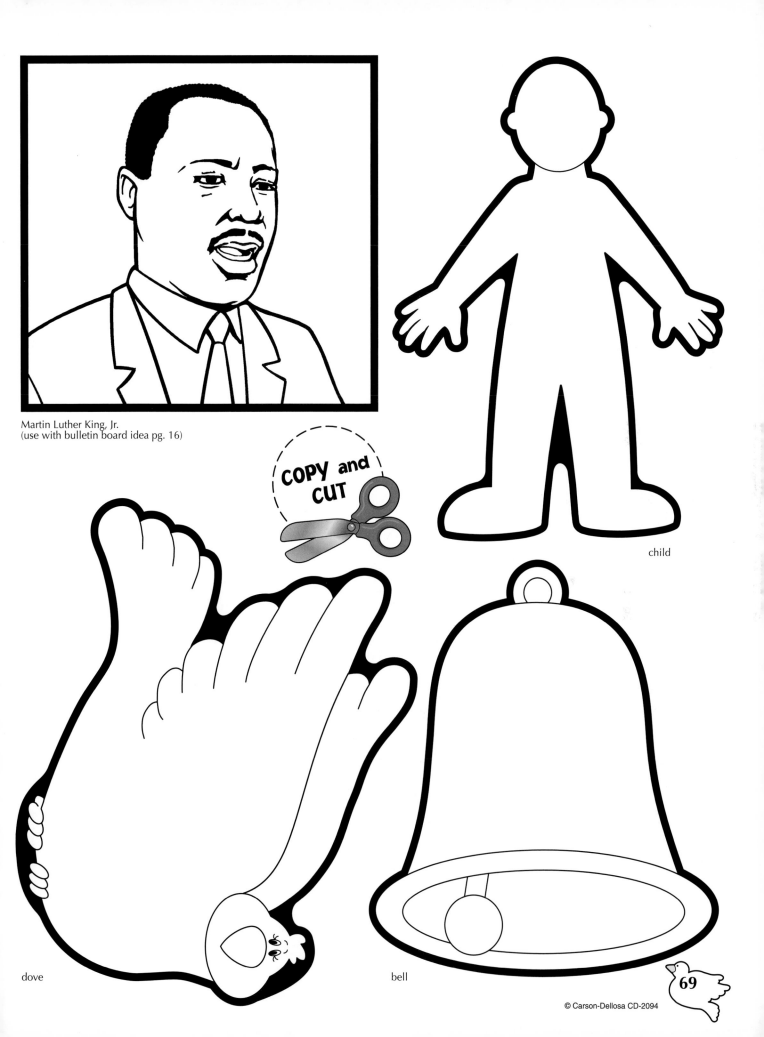

Martin Luther King, Jr.
(use with bulletin board idea pg. 16)

COPY and CUT

child

dove

bell

69

Once Upon a Time

Magic, adventure, and happy endings have kept people interested in fairy tales for centuries. Celebrate the birthdays of two famous recorders of fairy tales, Charles Perrault (January 13, 1628) and Jakob Grimm (January 4, 1785).

Did You Know?

- Fairy tales come from a tradition of oral storytelling and have been retold, changed, and added to over the years. There are no true authors of traditional fairy tales, only those credited with writing them down.
- Charles Perrault, a Frenchman, was one of the first people to write down a collection of fairy tales. His book, *Stories of My Mother Goose*, introduced the character of Mother Goose, now associated with nursery rhymes, to children's literature. German brothers Jakob and Wilhelm Karl Grimm felt it was important to record stories as closely as possible to the way they were told, so they interviewed German country people and wrote down the stories as they told them.
- Fairy tales were originally called nursery tales, but became fairy tales when Andrew Lang compiled several books of nursery tales called *The Blue Fairy Book*, *The Red Fairy Book*, etc.
- Hans Christian Andersen was the first to write original or "literary" fairy tales. A literary fairy tale is not written from a story that has been orally passed down through generations.

Literature Selections

The Random House Book of Fairy Tales by Amy Ehrlich: Random House, 1985. (Storybook, 208 pg.) Nineteen fairy tales including *Little Red Riding Hood*, *Cinderella*, and *Jack and the Beanstalk*.

The Jolly Postman or Other People's Letters by Allan and Janet Ahlberg: Little, Brown & Company, 1986. (Interactive book, 32 pg.) Inside envelopes are letters to characters that can be pulled out and read.

The Stinky Cheese Man and Other Fairly Stupid Tales by Jon Scieszka: Penguin Putnam Books, 1992. (Picture book, 56 pg.) Crazy, mixed-up fairy tales are paired with Caldecott honored illustrations.

Who Said That?

Write famous fairy tale quotes on the fronts of index cards, such as "Not by the hair of my chinny chin chin" or "Grandma, what big ears you have!" Write the names of the characters who said the quotes on the backs. Challenge students to guess the fairy tale characters. Then, let students make up their own quotes, writing a line that a fairy tale character might have said. For example, Cinderella might have said, "Where is my other shoe?" Let each student share his quote and let classmates guess the character.

Happily Ever After

Most fairy tales end with *and they lived happily ever after*. Ask students to think about what that might mean for a particular fairy tale. If Cinderella, for example, lived happily ever after, what was her life like? Did she become a famous doctor? Let each student pick a fairy tale and write a sequel to it. Have them tell what happens to the main characters after the traditional story ends. Students may choose to put a twist on *happily ever after* by adding, *or so they thought....*

Telling Tales

Fairy tales, like many traditional stories, are passed down through oral retellings. Because people remember stories differently and add their own details to fill in parts they have forgotten, fairy tales may have many different versions. Show students how this works by telling a short story and asking students to write the story down as they remember it. Let students read their versions, then compare the differences.

Map It Out

Create a wipe-off fairy tale story map that can be used throughout the unit. Write the information on a large piece of white poster board. Laminate the board and use an overhead pen or dry erase marker to help students fill in the blanks after reading a fairy tale. Encourage students to look for common themes and elements. If desired, create a worksheet like the board for students to complete on their own. The worksheets can be compiled at the end of the unit into a fairy tale reference book.

Cinderella

Cinderella by Charles Perrault: Atheneum, 1971. (Picture book, 32 pg.) Translation of Perrault's original French story. Illustrations by Marcia Brown won the Caldecott medal in 1955.
Yeh-Shen: A Cinderella Story from China by Ai-Ling Louie: Penguin Putnam Books, 1985. (Picture book, 32 pg.)
Sootface: An Ojibwa Indian Tale by Robert D. San Souci: Bantam Doubleday Dell Publishing Group, 1994. (Picture book, 32 pg.)
Princess Furball by Charlotte Huck: Greenwillow books, 1989. (Picture book, 40 pg.)

Cinderella Similarities

More than 300 versions of the Cinderella story have been told around the world. Most of them involve the mistreatment of Cinderella and her marriage to a prince or king. Many also include some object, like a slipper or ring, that the Prince uses to identify Cinderella. Divide students into small groups and assign a version of the story to each group. Have the groups read their stories and act them out for the class, letting one member be the narrator. After each group performs its story, complete *If the Slipper Fits* (below).

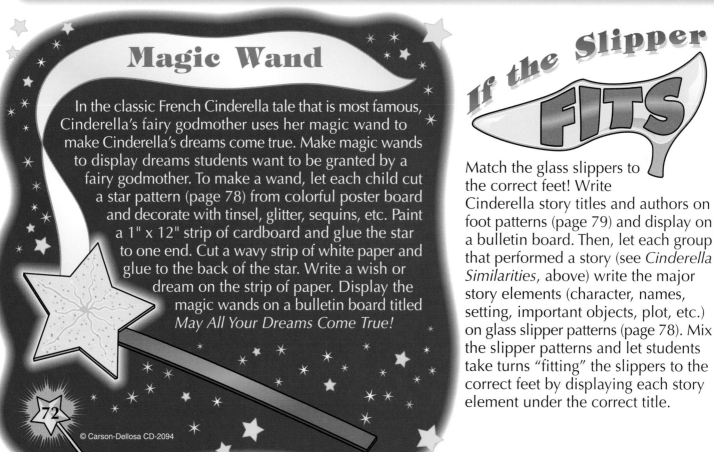

Magic Wand

In the classic French Cinderella tale that is most famous, Cinderella's fairy godmother uses her magic wand to make Cinderella's dreams come true. Make magic wands to display dreams students want to be granted by a fairy godmother. To make a wand, let each child cut a star pattern (page 78) from colorful poster board and decorate with tinsel, glitter, sequins, etc. Paint a 1" x 12" strip of cardboard and glue the star to one end. Cut a wavy strip of white paper and glue to the back of the star. Write a wish or dream on the strip of paper. Display the magic wands on a bulletin board titled *May All Your Dreams Come True!*

If the Slipper FITS

Match the glass slippers to the correct feet! Write Cinderella story titles and authors on foot patterns (page 79) and display on a bulletin board. Then, let each group that performed a story (see *Cinderella Similarities*, above) write the major story elements (character, names, setting, important objects, plot, etc.) on glass slipper patterns (page 78). Mix the slipper patterns and let students take turns "fitting" the slippers to the correct feet by displaying each story element under the correct title.

Little Red Riding Hood

Little Red Riding Hood by the Brothers Grimm: Troll Communications L.L.C., 1996. (Picture book, 32 pg.)
Lon Po Po: A Red-Riding Hood Story from China by Ed Young: Scholastic, Inc., 1989. (Picture book, 32 pg.)
Red Riding Hood by James Marshall: Scholastic, Inc., 1987. (Picture book, 32 pg.)

Goodies for Grandma

Help Little Red Riding Hood guess if Grandma is real or the Wolf by putting clues in her goody basket. Instruct each student to color and cut out a basket pattern (page 79), then trace around it on plain paper and cut it out. Staple the top of the basket to the top of the plain paper cut-out. Ask each child to decide whether her basket will contain clues for Grandma or the Wolf. Have students draw clues on the plain paper cut-out. The Wolf, for example, might have a wig and whisker trimmers and Grandma might have knitting needles and a framed photo of Little Red Riding Hood. Display the goody baskets and let students look "inside" them and guess to whom they belong.

Compare Stories

Little Red Riding Hood and *Lon Po Po* are surprisingly similar stories. Write matching aspects of both stories on sentence strips, such as the mother's advice, the questions the children ask the wolf about his appearance, how the wolf is killed, etc. *The mother went to visit Po Po*, for example, would match *Little Red Riding Hood went to visit grandma*. Mix the sentence strips in a pocket chart or on a bulletin board and let students take turns matching the corresponding elements from both stories.

What Big Ears You Have!

Let students participate in the reading of *Little Red Riding Hood*. Give students construction paper, paint, felt, etc., to make big wolf ears, eyes, hands, and sharp teeth to hold over their own ears, eyes, etc., during the appropriate parts of the story. Encourage students to respond as the wolf ("the better to hear you with, my dear!").

73

The Three Little Javelinas by Susan Lowell: Northland Publishing, 1992. (Picture book, 32 pg.)

The Three Little Pigs by Paul Galdone: Clarion Books, 1970. (Picture book, 48 pg.)

The True Story of the 3 Little Pigs by Jon Scieszka: Scholastic, Inc., 1989. (Picture book, 32 pg.)

Build a Comparison

Read *The Three Little Pigs* by Paul Galdone and *The Three Little Javelinas* by Susan Lowell, then give each student three enlarged house patterns (page 79). Glue the houses in a row on a strip of green construction paper. Label one pattern *The Three Little Pigs*, another *The Three Little Javelinas*, and the last *Same*. Decorate the roofs of the houses to look like the three houses the pigs build in the story by gluing on bits of wheat biscuit cereal, toothpicks, and small red construction paper rectangles. Write details about each story that are different on the appropriate houses and details that are the same on the other house. Let students draw and cut out three pigs and a wolf to glue to the scene.

Wolf-Proof Houses

Ask students to be creative by designing completely wolf-proof houses. Have each student draw a diagram of the house on plain paper, labeling each feature that will keep the Big Bad Wolf away. Let students share their houses with the class, then display the houses on a bulletin board titled *Not By the Hairs of Our Chinny Chin Chins!*

That's Not the Way I See It

Fairy tales are traditionally told from a narrator's perspective. Read *The True Story of the 3 Little Pigs* by Jon Scieszka and talk about how A. Wolf saw things differently than the narrator of the traditional story. Then, challenge students to rewrite a fairy tale from another character's perspective. Because fairy tales are narrated, they can be rewritten from any of the main characters' perspectives. Compile the completed stories into a class book.

Rumpelstiltskin

Rumpelstiltskin by Paul O. Zelinsky: E.P. Dutton, 1986. (Picture book, 38 pg.)
Rumpelstiltskin by Paul Galdone: Clarion Books, 1985. (Picture book, 34 pg.)
Rumpelstiltskin by the Brothers Grimm: Troll Communications L.L.C., 1979. (Picture book, 32 pg.)

Guess My Name Game

Rumpelstiltskin had a silly sounding name that was hard to guess. Have each student scramble the letters in his name to make up a silly name that is hard to guess. For example, if his name were Sam, his silly name could be Ams. Write each silly name on an index card, number it, and display in a pocket chart. Let students number a piece of paper according to the number of names in the pocket chart and try to figure out each name during free time. Reward the first child to guess all of the names correctly with a coupon for free time, a homework pass, gold chocolate coins, etc.

Spin a Tale

Spin a fairy tale into a golden summary. Give each child an enlarged copy of the spinning wheel pattern (page 78). Have him write a summary of the story around the spinning wheel, starting at the spindle, circling the wheel (several times, if necessary), and ending back at the spindle. Glue the spinning wheel to construction paper and add a pile of straw or raffia on the paper around it. Accent the completed picture and spindle with gold glitter.

Which Character Has Character

Admirable character traits are found in an unlikely character... Rumpelstiltskin! Many people say Rumpelstiltskin is the villain in this fairy tale, but is he? Have students examine the character traits, based on the character's actions, for each character in the story. Write the name of each character on the board with a list of character traits, such as compassion, fairness, honesty, trustworthiness, perseverance, etc. Using the story as reference, have students decide whether each character shows each trait. Students will be surprised to find that Rumpelstiltskin demonstrated several character traits including compassion, trustworthiness, and fairness. Based on these facts, have students reevaluate who they think is the villain of the story.

75

Jack and the Beanstalk

Jack and the Beanstalk Stories

Jack and the Beanstalk by Matt Faulkner: Scholastic, Inc., 1986. (Picture book, 32 pg.)
Jack and the Beanstalk by Ann K. Beneduce: Penguin Putnam Books, 1999. (Picture book, 32 pg.)
Jack and the Beanstalk by Steven Kellogg: Morrow/Avon, 1991. (Picture book, 48 pg.)

Jack on Trial

The main character in a fairy tale is called the hero, but was Jack really a hero or just a thief? Set up a mock courtroom and put Jack on trial for robbery. Assign students to be witnesses, jury members, the judge, lawyers, etc. Present opening statements, evidence, witnesses (mother, bean seller, Giant's wife, Giant), and "retell" the story during the trial. Then, let Jack speak in his own defense. Jurors can decide a verdict and, if necessary, the judge can decide a sentence for Jack.

Grow a Story

Make a "growing" vine booklet that tells the story of *Jack and the Beanstalk*. Fold a 3" x 18" strip of green construction paper accordion-style into six sections. Cut six green leaves using the leaf pattern (page 78) and glue one to each accordion section so that it overlaps the edge. Break the story into six major events and write each on a leaf, starting with the bottom leaf. Cut brown paper to glue to the bottom of the vine and on it write *Jack and the Beanstalk*.

If I Planted Magic Beans

Encourage students to imagine what might happen if they planted magic beans, then have them write stories describing the beanstalks and what would be at the tops of the beanstalks. Let students make the stories into books. Fold a sheet of 18" x 12" construction paper in half, write the title of the story, and glue on dried beans. Place the pages inside the cover, punch holes along the left side and tie with yarn to bind. Have each child draw a beanstalk on a strip of green paper, then accordion fold the strip and glue one end to the inside cover of the book. Draw a small picture of what was on top of the beanstalk and glue it to the other end of the strip. Students can unfold the strips to reveal the beanstalks during the reading. Let students exchange books and read each others' stories.

If I Planted Some Magic Beans

The Ugly Duckling

Ugly Duckling Stories

The Ugly Duckling retold by Adrian Mitchell: Kindersley Publishing, Inc., 1994. (Picture book, 32 pg.)
The Ugly Duckling by Hans Christian Andersen: Charles Scribner's Sons, 1965. (Story book, 48 pg.)
The Ugly Duckling adapted by Jerry Pinkney: Morrow Junior Books, 1999. (Picture book, 32 pg.)

Advice to the Ugly Duckling

5¢

Write an imaginary letter from the Ugly Duckling on a sheet of chart paper and display for the class to read. Write the letter as if the duckling is seeking advice, for example, *I hate the way I look. I don't fit in with my brothers and sisters. Everyone laughs at me because I'm different. I feel terrible about myself. What can I do?* Let the children write letters of advice to the Ugly Duckling telling him how to feel better about himself. Share the completed letters and display them on a bulletin board around the original letter.

Transformation Puppet

Create ugly duckling puppets that transform into beautiful swans. Glue felt and feathers to a white sock to make an ugly duckling. When dry, turn the sock inside out and make a beautiful swan. Let each child tell the story of the Ugly Duckling in her own words, using her puppet to show the action. Other props can be made, including a reflective pond made from aluminum foil wrapped over poster board. Brown socks can be made into ducks and children can act out the story.

Write and Publish

Why Dogs and Cats Don't Like Each Other

Hans Christian Andersen wrote *The Ugly Duckling* and many other original fairy tales. Challenge students to write original fairy tales of their own. Let them use the story map from *Map It Out* (page 71) to help them plot out the basic elements of their fairy tales. When the fairy tales are complete, have students divide their stories into major events and write each event on a separate page. Then, illustrate each page on a separate sheet of paper. Arrange the text and illustrations in order, then glue the text for the next page to the back of the illustration for the previous page. Cut poster board for the front and back covers, punch holes through all layers of the book, and bind with gold ribbon or sparkly pipe cleaners. Invite a younger class to a fairy tale reading and let students share their original literary works!

77

glass slipper

COPY and CUT

spinning wheel

leaf

star

78

© Carson-Dellosa CD-2094

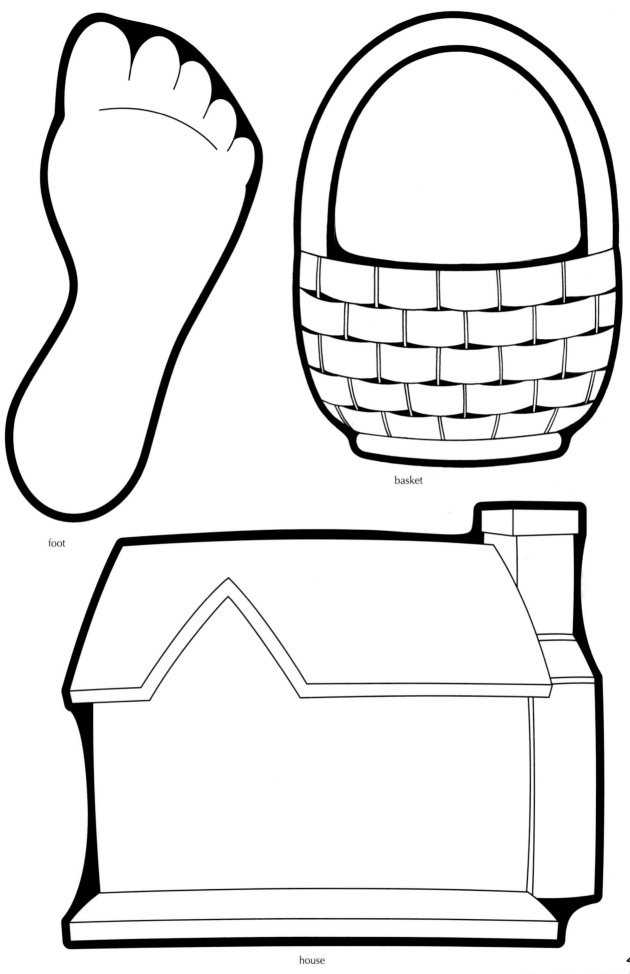

foot

basket

house

79

PEOPLE OF THE ARCTIC

Introduce students to the traditional way of life of the Arctic Inuit and Sami people. Although life for these groups has changed with modern times, most families continue to teach younger generations the customs and traditions of their ancestors.

DID YOU KNOW?

The Inuit (IN•yu•wut)

- The Inuit lived in several different kinds of homes, all of which are called igloos. Wooden houses that were above ground, wood and sod houses that were partially underground, or homes made from stone and turf were built depending on the season and the region where the group lived.
- Inuit legends tell how the polar bear taught them to hunt and keep warm. Inuits probably learned to hunt seals by watching polar bears. The snowhouses built by Inuit hunters were probably modeled after polar bear dens.

The Sami (SAW•mee)

- At one time, the Sami followed the migration of reindeer herds, traveling with them from winter pastures to summer feeding grounds. Reindeer were the main source of food for the Sami.
- The Sami invented skis as a travel method. The word *ski* comes from the word *skridfinrna* (skreed•FEEN•rr•na), which is a Scandinavian word for Lapland, the name of the area where the Sami live.
- The Sami have many words for reindeer in their language, Lappish. There are words which describe the size, age, and appearance of reindeer, and special words to describe the shapes of reindeer antlers.

LITERATURE SELECTIONS

Arctic Son by Jean Craighead George: Hyperion Books for Children, 1997. (Picture book, 32 pg.) An English boy grows up living and learning the customs of the Eskimo people in Alaska.

Lapps—Reindeer Herders of Lapland by Alan James: Rourke Publications, Inc., 1989. (Student reference book, 48 pg.) Describes the culture, customs and daily life of the Sami, or Lapps.

Very Last First Time by Jan Andrews: Simon & Schuster Children's Books, 1998. (Picture book, 32 pg.) An Inuit girl climbs below the sea ice to collect mussels by herself for the first time.

LIFE IN THE ARCTIC

The Inuit and the Sami, or Lapps, are native peoples of the Arctic. The Inuit live in regions of Alaska, Canada, Greenland, Siberia, and northern Labrador. The Sami are native to the northernmost parts of Russia, Finland, Sweden, and Norway, the area known as *Lapland*. Compare and contrast the Inuit and the Sami. Provide several 5" x 8" index cards labeled *Inuit* or *Sami* on the backs. Divide the class into two groups and assign students to write about and illustrate the clothing, homes, modes of transportation, or food for the group named on their cards. On chart paper, label one column *Inuit* and the other *Sami*. Let each student present the information on his card, then place the card in the correct column.

Inuit
Live in igloos

Sami
Live in kåtas

The Inuit

Snowhouses

An Inuit family living in the coldest regions of the Arctic during the winter built an *igluviak* (i•GLOO•vi•ak), or snowhouse. An igluviak was a dome-shaped shelter made from blocks of tightly packed snow. A small tunnel that could be blocked with snow to keep cold air out was connected to the front of the igluviak . A soapstone lamp fueled by whale blubber was placed in the center of the igluviak for warmth and light. The Inuit built platforms off the ground and close to the top of the dome where it was warmest. They slept, cooked, and worked on these platforms. Sometimes several igluviak were connected by underground tunnels so people could travel between them without going outside. Have each child sponge paint an igluviak using white paint, sponges, and construction paper. After each student has painted an igluviak on paper, cut out the igluviak and glue the top edge to a piece of blue paper. Have students lift up the igluviak, draw a scene on the blue paper, then write about the scene inside.

Animal Carvings

The Inuit used soapstone, bone, and ivory to carve images of Arctic animals. Before carving the design, the artist would hold the stone, piece of bone, or ivory and think about what to carve. Let each child create an animal carving using a bar of soap and a spoon (Ivory® or Dove® work well). Lightly draw an outline of the animal on the soap and use the edge of the spoon to shape the design. When the carving is complete, smooth it by rubbing a damp cloth over the surface.

Guessing Game

Because Inuit families were indoors most of the winter, they spent time playing games. One game involved one group guessing which carved pieces a second group was hiding under a blanket. Play a version of this game. Divide students into two teams. Enlarge the guessing game patterns (page 83) on heavy paper or allow students to use their soap carvings from *Animal Carvings* (above). Have students sit in two rows with a large blanket between them. Have the first group turn their backs to the second group. Give each member of the second group a pattern to hold under the blanket. Then, instruct a member from the first group to face the second group, choose a player, and guess which pattern that player is holding under the blanket. If a student guesses correctly, have the player place the pattern on the blanket. Continue the game until each pattern has been revealed. The team to identify all the patterns with the fewest guesses wins.

THE SAMI

COLORFUL CLOTHING

A traditional feature of the Sami is their bright and colorful clothing. Sami men wear large hats with a flap of fabric at the top. Sami women wear bonnets with ear flaps. A tunic called a *kolte* (kol•TEE) is made of blue fabric accented with blue, red, green, and yellow bands of embroidery. The embroidered designs are very detailed and often incorporate flowers. Allow students to decorate the Sami hat and Sami bonnet patterns (page 83) using blue, yellow, red, and green pencils. Provide scraps of ricrac, ribbon, and felt to accent the hats and bonnets.

REINDEER GAMES

During spring, the Sami often visited other families in nearby villages. Reindeer contests were held during these get-togethers, including reindeer-lassoing and reindeer sled racing. Have children play a version of a Sami reindeer game. Pair students and have one act as the reindeer and the other as a passenger in the sled. Instruct each "reindeer" to stand in front of each "passenger" with his arms extended behind him. Let the passenger stand behind the reindeer and hold the "reindeer's" hands. Set up two obstacle courses and have two reindeer compete to pull their passengers through the course as quickly as they can.

BUILDING A KÅTA

The Sami had to travel often when following the reindeer herds. Each family built a large *kåta*, or tent, that could be quickly pitched or packed. A kåta was made by covering wooden poles with reindeer skins or sheets of canvas. A fire was usually kept burning inside the kåta, so an opening was left at the top to allow smoke to escape. Have each student make a kåta with 8" twigs and grocery bags. Give each child several twigs. Instruct students to bunch the twigs together at one end, then glue them on construction paper. Provide brown grocery bags and have each student cut a tent shape from a bag. Glue the tent shape over the twigs. Cut a flap in front of the tent and draw a Sami family inside the kåta.

seal	walrus	polar bear	fish
sled dog	whale	narwhal	caribou
puffin	arctic fox	arctic hare	musk ox

guessing game patterns

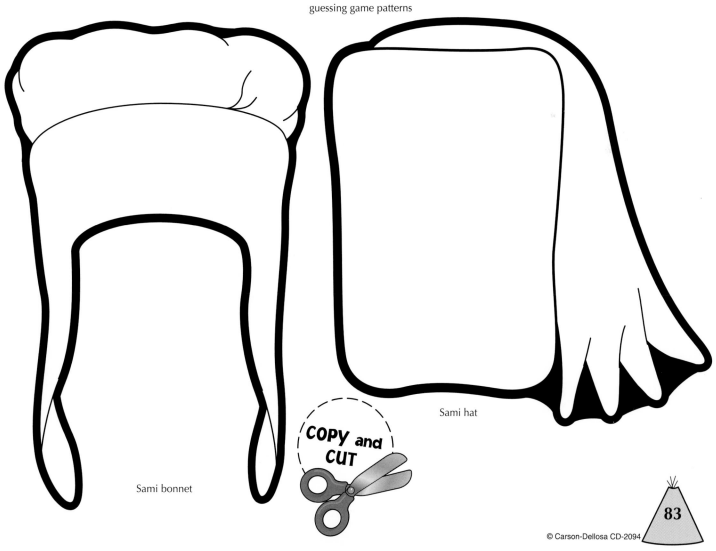

Sami bonnet

COPY and CUT

Sami hat

Benjamin Franklin

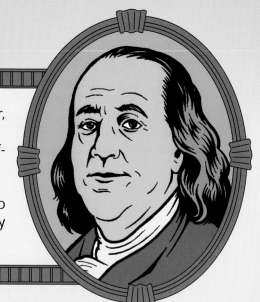

Benjamin Franklin, inventor, statesman, diplomat, printer, writer, citizen, and scientist, was born on January 17, 1706. Most of his knowledge, including music and foreign languages, was self-taught. He is most famous for his kite and key experiment, proving that lightning is electricity. Benjamin Franklin's experiments with electricity paved the way for later inventors to create many of the useful applications of electricity that we enjoy today such as lightbulbs and batteries.

Did You Know?

Benjamin Franklin helped make Philadelphia, Pennsylvania one of the most advanced cities in America at the time, establishing a lending library, volunteer fire department, fire insurance company, hospital, university, and street cleaning department. He also made significant improvements in the postal system during his service as postmaster of Philadelphia and of the United States.

Benjamin Franklin was a generous man who never asked for money for his inventions. He donated his salary as postmaster to wounded soldiers of the Revolutionary War and left large sums of money in his will to the cities of Boston, Massachusetts and Philadelphia, Pennsylvania to be used for public works.

Part of the money Benjamin Franklin left to Philadelphia was used to establish the Franklin Institute, which is dedicated to making science accessible to everyone. Many of Franklin's original inventions are displayed today at the Franklin Institute.

Benjamin Franklin's picture is found on the one hundred dollar bill.

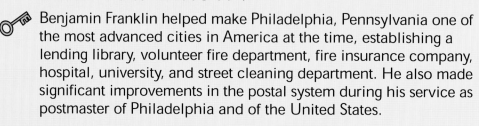

Literature Selections

Poor Richard's Almanack for Kids by Benjamin Franklin: New Hope Press, 1994 (Reference book, 64 pg.) Includes famous quotations from Benjamin Franklin.

The Many Lives of Benjamin Franklin by Aliki: Prentice Hall, Inc., 1977. (Picture book, 32 pg.) Extols the many accomplishments of Benjamin Franklin during his lifetime.

A Picture Book of Benjamin Franklin by David Adler: Holiday House, 1990. (Picture book, 32 pg.) An easy to understand biography of Benjamin Franklin.

Jack of All Trades

Most people remember Franklin for his experiments with electricity, but he accomplished much more during his lifetime. Divide students into five groups and assign each group an aspect of Franklin's life to research: inventor, scientist, community advocate, publisher/writer, and statesman/diplomat. Write each category on an enlarged key pattern (page 88) and have each group write its research on enlarged kite patterns (page 88). Display each kite with its key on a bulletin board titled *Benjamin Franklin's Enlightening Life.*

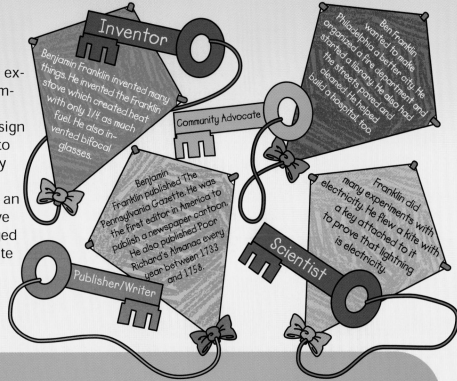

Inventor
Benjamin Franklin invented many things. He invented the Franklin stove which created heat with only 1/4 as much fuel. He also invented bifocal glasses.

Community Advocate
Ben Franklin wanted to make Philadelphia a better city. He organized a fire department and started a library. He also had the streets paved and cleaned. He helped build a hospital, too.

Publisher/Writer
Benjamin Franklin published The Pennsylvania Gazette. He was the first editor in America to publish a newspaper cartoon. He also published Poor Richard's Almanac every year between 1733 and 1758.

Scientist
Franklin did many experiments with electricity. He flew a kite with a key attached to it to prove that lightning is electricity.

Class Almanac

Benjamin Franklin wrote and published *Poor Richard's Almanack* each year from 1733 to 1758 under the pen name of Richard Saunders who was, supposedly, a poor astrologer. The almanac featured advice, wise sayings, humor, poetry, philosophy, and weather and astronomical predictions. Create a class almanac to give advice, document events throughout the year, etc., for next year's class to read. For example, encourage students to write their own sayings, poems, and philosophies for getting along in second grade. Let each student sign her work with her own name or make up a pen name. Compile the completed pages in a three-ring binder so students can add pages to the almanac throughout the year.

Community Advocate

Benjamin Franklin saw a need for many things in his city, such as a fire department, a library, and a hospital. He thought it was a person's civic duty to work to improve the community. Ask students to think of things that would make their school or classroom a better place, such as a playground or a volunteer homework help center. Encourage students to think of new and different ideas and write the ideas on key patterns (page 88). Let students draw a map of the school on butcher paper and attach the keys to the map where they would best be suited. Post the map on a wall or bulletin board titled *The Keys to a Better School.*

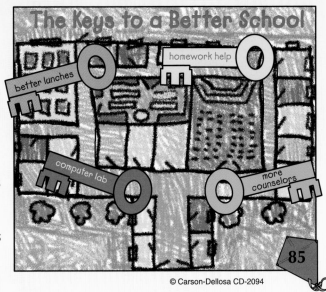

The Keys to a Better School

better lunches

homework help

computer lab

more counselors

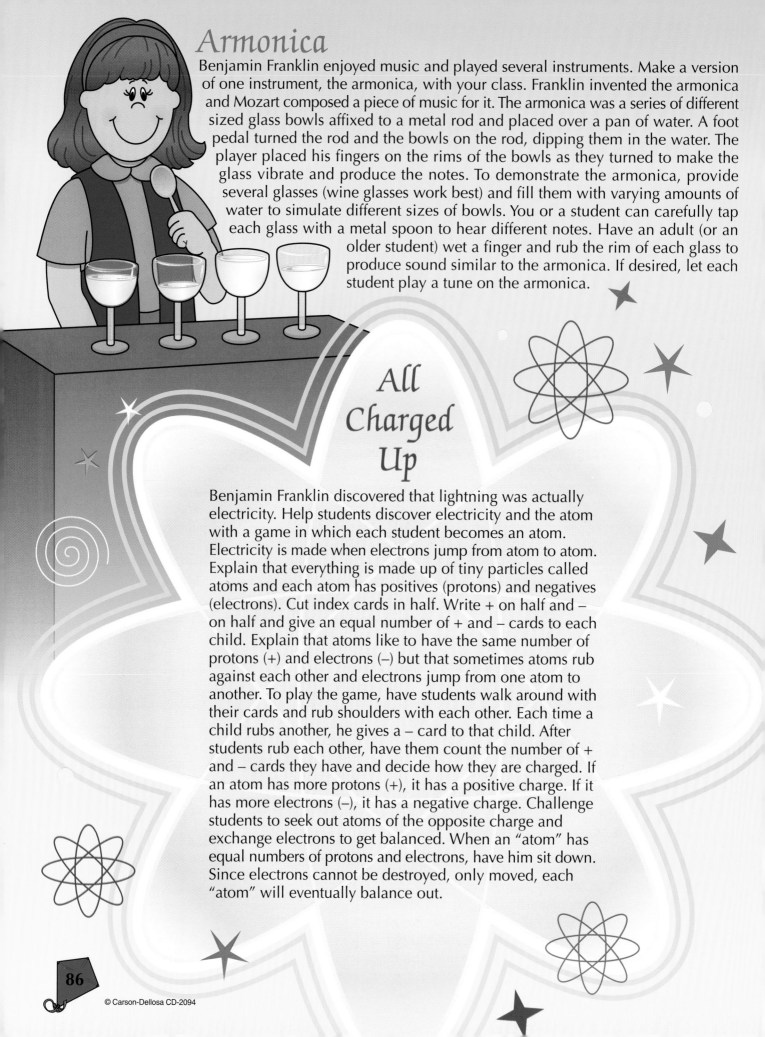

Armonica

Benjamin Franklin enjoyed music and played several instruments. Make a version of one instrument, the armonica, with your class. Franklin invented the armonica and Mozart composed a piece of music for it. The armonica was a series of different sized glass bowls affixed to a metal rod and placed over a pan of water. A foot pedal turned the rod and the bowls on the rod, dipping them in the water. The player placed his fingers on the rims of the bowls as they turned to make the glass vibrate and produce the notes. To demonstrate the armonica, provide several glasses (wine glasses work best) and fill them with varying amounts of water to simulate different sizes of bowls. You or a student can carefully tap each glass with a metal spoon to hear different notes. Have an adult (or an older student) wet a finger and rub the rim of each glass to produce sound similar to the armonica. If desired, let each student play a tune on the armonica.

All Charged Up

Benjamin Franklin discovered that lightning was actually electricity. Help students discover electricity and the atom with a game in which each student becomes an atom. Electricity is made when electrons jump from atom to atom. Explain that everything is made up of tiny particles called atoms and each atom has positives (protons) and negatives (electrons). Cut index cards in half. Write + on half and – on half and give an equal number of + and – cards to each child. Explain that atoms like to have the same number of protons (+) and electrons (–) but that sometimes atoms rub against each other and electrons jump from one atom to another. To play the game, have students walk around with their cards and rub shoulders with each other. Each time a child rubs another, he gives a – card to that child. After students rub each other, have them count the number of + and – cards they have and decide how they are charged. If an atom has more protons (+), it has a positive charge. If it has more electrons (–), it has a negative charge. Challenge students to seek out atoms of the opposite charge and exchange electrons to get balanced. When an "atom" has equal numbers of protons and electrons, have him sit down. Since electrons cannot be destroyed, only moved, each "atom" will eventually balance out.

Kite and Key

Ben Franklin proved lightning is a big spark of static electricity with his kite and key experiment in 1752. Let each student learn this principle by creating a mobile of Franklin's experiment. Explain that the small spark that results when you rub your feet across carpet and touch a doorknob is static electricity. Electrons in the carpet rub off and spread out over your body. When you touch the doorknob, the electrons jump off your body and into the doorknob, creating a spark of electricity or mini lightning bolt.

With lightning, the cloud (charged by water and ice particles rubbing together) is like your body after walking across the carpet, and the Earth is like the doorknob. The electric charge in a storm cloud is much stronger than the charge your body gets from carpet, so the cloud does not need to touch the ground for electrons to jump from the cloud to the ground. When Franklin flew his kite, he gathered an electric charge from the storm clouds. The charge traveled down the kite string to the key. When he touched the key, a spark of electricity was formed.

Make a mobile of Franklin's kite experiment to show the path of the electric charge from the storm cloud to the key. Cut out a cloud shape from gray paper, three lightning bolts from yellow paper, an enlarged kite pattern (page 88), and a key pattern (page 88). Glue the kite to the cloud. Then, glue the lightning bolts behind the cloud. Tape yarn to the bottom of the kite and tie the key to the other end. Punch two holes in the cloud top and tie yarn through the holes for hanging.

Static Magic

In the 1700's, scientists thought there were two different kinds of electricity, but Franklin believed there was only one kind and it could be positive or negative. Let your students come to the same conclusion Franklin did with these static electricity experiments.

Franklin discovered that objects with the same charge repel each other. Show this by electrically charging rubber balloons. Blow up two balloons and tie a 12" string to each. Tie the strings together and hold the string at the knot. Rub each balloon briskly with a wool scarf or sweater. The balloons should be forced apart because they both have negative charges.

Franklin also discovered that objects with opposite charges attract each other. Demonstrate by giving each child 10-15 plastic foam packing chips and a balloon. Instruct students to rub their balloons against wool or their hair, then hold the balloons over the packing chips and watch the charged balloons pick up the chips. (This works best on cold, dry days.) Let students experiment with like charges by gently pushing the chips over the surface of the balloon, and discovering that the chips jump away from each other.

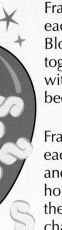

87

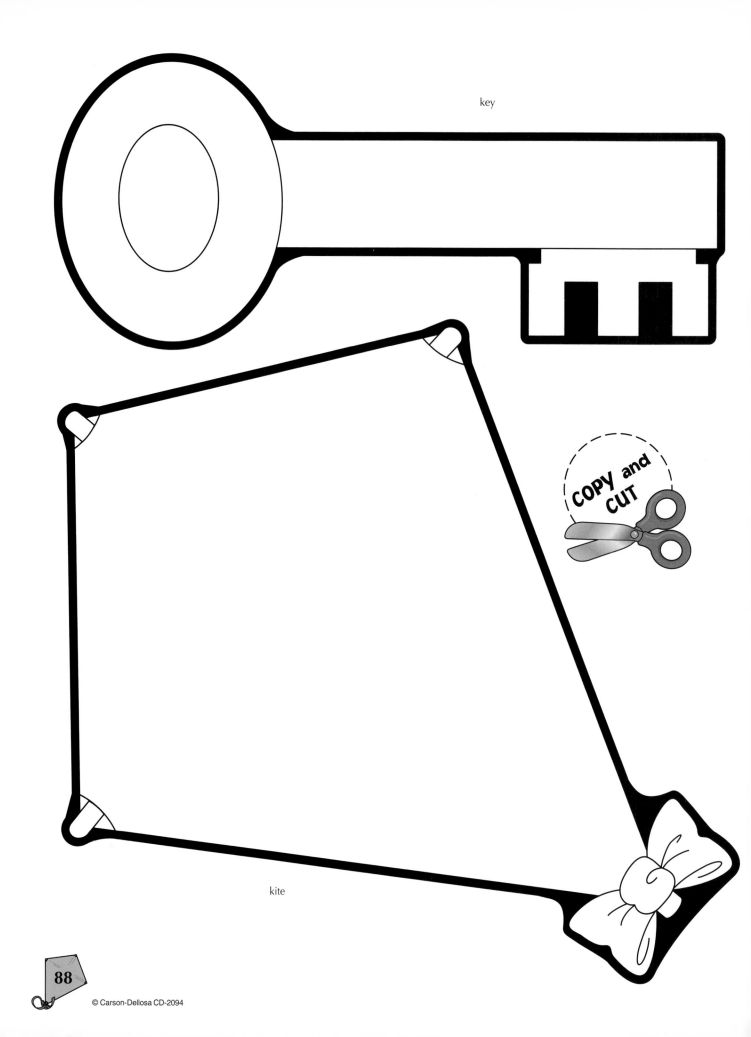

key

COPY and CUT

kite

Hats Off To Hats

National Hat Day is celebrated on the third Friday in January. Make hats "tops" with these fun activities!

Did You Know?

People in different world regions often make hats from indigenous materials: reindeer fur in Siberia, palm leaves in Puerto Rico, seashells in New Guinea, and tropical flowers in Bali.

Throughout history, tall hats have represented wealth and status in many cultures. The early kings of Egypt wore tall hats made from reeds wrapped in cloth. More recently, top hats were worn by wealthy Europeans and Americans.

In some countries, family members wear the same style hat in a specific pattern. Some have even worn the same style for hundreds, or thousands, of years.

Literature Selections

The Extraordinary Adventures of an Ordinary Hat by Wolfram Hamel: North-South Books, Inc., 1995. (Story book, 64 pg.) A black hat is purchased and travels into the world.

The Hat by Jan Brett: Penguin Putnam Books for Young Readers, 1997. (Picture book, 32 pg.) Hedgie the Hedgehog fashions himself a winter hat from a red and white woolen stocking.

Caps for Sale by Esphyr Slobodkina: HarperCollins Children's Books, 1996. (Picture book, 48 pg.) A cap peddler's caps are taken by monkeys.

A Three Hat Day by Laura Geringer: HarperCollins Children's Books, 1987. (Picture book, 32 pg.) See how a hat collector meet his perfect match.

Craft Your Own Hat

Let students show off their own hat styles. Give each child a sheet of newspaper. Instruct students to fold the paper in half horizontally and turn the paper so the fold is at the top. Fold the top corners down and tape the points. Fold up the bottom edges and tape the sides. Provide feathers, paint, sequins, and glitter and allow students to decorate their hats.

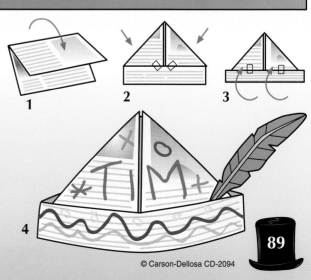

1 2 3 4

International Hats

Hats come in many shapes, sizes, colors, and styles. Teach students about hats from different countries. Copy the hat patterns (page 91). Post the patterns around a world map. Have students research and write information about each hat, the country from which it comes, and who wears it. Let students connect the hat patterns to the correct countries with string. Post the reports beside the corresponding hat patterns on the bulletin board.

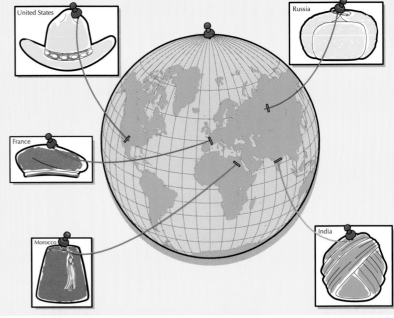

Who Wears That Hat?

Create an interactive hat vocabulary game for students to enjoy! Enlarge the community helper hat patterns (page 92), attach each pattern to a strip of oak tag, then attach the oak tag to a craft stick. Place a hat behind a student's head without her seeing which hat it is. Then, have classmates give the student clues to help her guess which hat she is "wearing".

Mexican Hat Dance

A sombrero is a Mexican hat with a tall tapered crown and a wide brim. Its name comes from the word *sombre* which means *shade*. Let students practice a traditional Mexican Hat Dance. Place a large sombrero in the middle of the floor (or use a large paper circle decorated like a sombrero). Have students form a circle around the sombrero. If you have a large class, you may need to use more than one hat. Play a recording of the *Mexican Hat Dance*, and ask students to move clockwise around the hat, stomping their feet and clapping their hands. To mimic the traditional dance, students should actually try to touch the rim of the hat with their feet as they move around it.

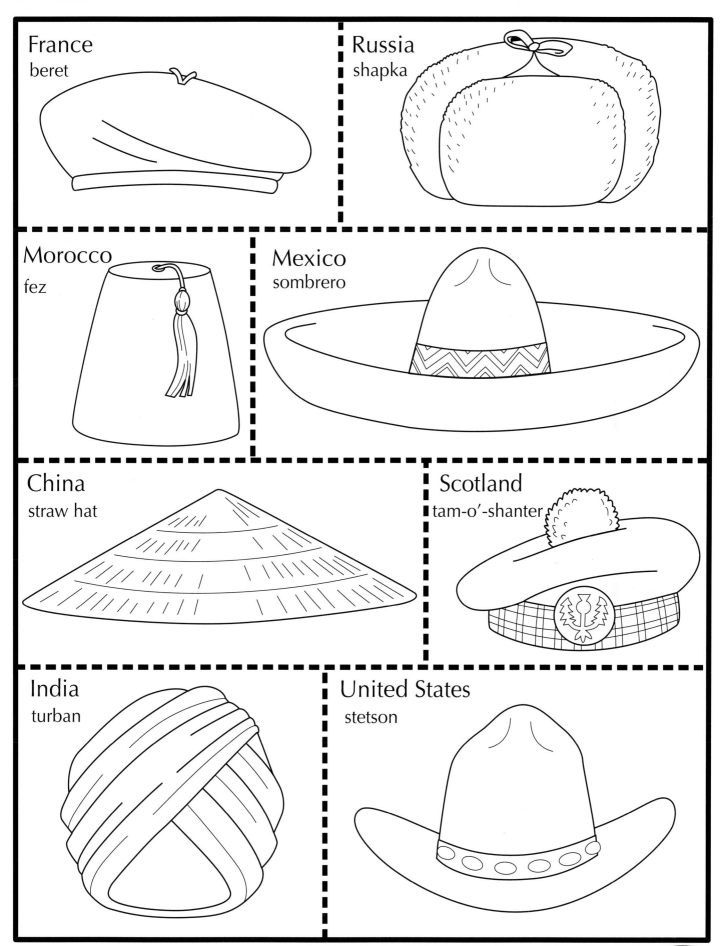

France
beret

Russia
shapka

Morocco
fez

Mexico
sombrero

China
straw hat

Scotland
tam-o'-shanter

India
turban

United States
stetson

Only one country has been represented for each hat.

91

firefighter's hat

construction worker's hat

nurse's hat

baseball player's hat

police officer's hat

chef's hat

forest ranger's hat

COPY and CUT

FD
9

CONSTRUCTION

INTERNATIONAL

Holidays

Ramadan

Ramadan is the ninth month of the Muslim calendar, which is based on the phases of the moon, and usually occurs in December or January. Muslims are followers of the Islam religion which is predominant in such countries as Jordan and Saudi Arabia. Ramadan is a sacred month for Muslims because it is the time when the *Koran* (the holy book of Islam) was revealed to the Prophet Mohammad. During Ramadan, Muslims fast from sunrise to sunset, which means they do not eat or drink anything. Ramadan is a time of contemplation and worship when Muslims concentrate on their faith and spend less time on everyday concerns.

Time to be Kind

Ramadan is also a time to be kind to friends, family, and strangers. Some Muslim families invite the less fortunate to share the feast of *Eid ul-Fitr*, which follows the month of Ramadan. Have each student make a pledge to do something kind during Ramadan. Let each student cut a heart shape from red paper. Then, have students trace their hands and cut them out. Glue the hands to the sides of the heart so that it looks like they are holding the heart. On his heart, have each student write and illustrate one kind thing he will do. Ask each student to complete his kind deed and describe it to the class.

> I will take my little sister to the park.
>
> Jeffrey

Date Bars

Muslims fast during Ramadan to show that they can enjoy life without overindulging. Dates are eaten in the evenings, breaking the fast, to follow the tradition set by Prophet Mohammad. To commemorate this, make date bars.

Ingredients

10 ounces of dates (pitted, dried, and chopped)
2/3 cup of water
2/3 cup of sugar
1/3 cup of lemon juice
2 prepared pie crusts

Preheat oven to 425°. Place the dates in the water and bring to a boil. Reduce heat to medium. Cook for five minutes until mixture is thick. Stir in sugar. Remove from heat and add lemon juice. Allow to cool. Grease a 9" x 9" baking pan. Place one pie crust in the pan. Cut the crust so it is flat in the pan. Pour the date mixture on top. Place the second crust on top of the date mixture. Slit the crust top with a knife. Bake for 35-40 minutes or until crust is brown. Let cool and cut into bars. Makes 9 bars.

DATES

93

Ramadan (continued)

Candy Bundles

At the end of Ramadan, Muslims celebrate Eid ul-Fitr, a festival of eating, giving food to the less fortunate, exchanging cards, and visiting friends and family. Many Muslims are excited and happy that another successful fast is over. To some Muslims, Eid-ul-Fitr is also known as "the candy holiday" since many children receive gifts of candy shaped as dolls or wrapped in colorful handkerchiefs. Let students join in the "sweet" side of this holiday by making candy bundles to keep or give as gifts. Give each student several large squares of tissue paper and a handful of wrapped candies. Have each student decorate a piece of tissue paper using felt tip markers, being careful not to tear the paper. Stack the tissue paper with the decorated paper at the bottom of the stack. Tell students to place their wrapped candies in the middle of their papers and twist the tissue papers around the candies. Provide students with ribbon or yarn to tie the papers together at the top. Students can keep the candy bundles or give them as gifts.

What Would you Wear?

During Eid-ul-Fitr, it is customary for people to dress in new clothes. Allow students to design their own new outfits. Give each student a piece of construction paper, glue, scissors, cloth scraps, sequins, etc. First, have each student draw a picture of himself on the construction paper. Then, cut clothes from the art materials and glue them to the self-portraits. Hang the pictures on a bulletin board titled *Dressing for the Occasion*.

Crescent Cookies

Muslims know when Ramadan begins and ends when they see that the crescent moon is visible in the sky. Celebrate the beginning of Eid-ul-Fitr with the class by making crescent moon cookies to enjoy. Bring refrigerated sugar cookie dough, crescent-shaped cookie cutters, a rolling pin, and a cookie sheet to class. Roll the dough on a clean, flat surface and allow each student to press the cookie cutter into the dough. Place the cookies on a cookie sheet and bake following the package directions. Have students talk about their favorite phases of the moon (new, crescent, half, full) while enjoying the cookies.

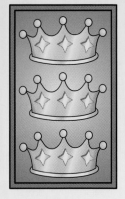

Epiphany

Epiphany, also known as Three Kings Day, is celebrated on January 6 in Spain and many other European countries. It is believed that the Three Kings who visited the baby Jesus Christ will also visit children and bring them gifts on this night. In Madrid, there is a parade in which the Three Kings throw candy to children who line the sidewalks.

Roscon Cake

Roscon, which means ring-shaped roll, is the traditional cake eaten on the morning of Epiphany. The cake looks like a doughnut-shaped fruit cake and is filled with cream or chocolate. The cake has a special toy baked inside and tradition says that whoever finds it will be lucky during the year. Have students create their own decorative roscon cakes in honor of Epiphany. Provide each student with a ring-shaped piece of cardboard or poster board. Let students cut fruit shapes from construction paper to glue to the rings. Provide gum drops for students to glue to their rings. Hang the roscon cakes on a bulletin board or wall. Tape small toys behind each cake and let students find their lucky prizes.

Royal Crowns

Students will think these wise men crowns are heads above the rest! Have students tape two pieces of construction paper together and decorate them with sequins, glitter, crayons, and markers. Wrap the construction paper around each students' head so that it fits comfortably, and tape the ends together to form a crown. Have students cut zigzag patterns into the tops of their crowns. If desired, let students wear their crowns and parade around the room.

Gifts for Everyone!

Most Spanish children leave their shoes out for the Three Kings to fill with presents, but the Kings usually put the presents all over the room. Play a game of *Find the Present* with the class. Provide each student with two pieces of construction paper, tape, and yarn. Have each student trace two copies of one foot on the construction paper and cut them out. Then, cut the heel off one cut-out and punch four holes in the center. Lace the yarn through the holes and tie it to resemble a shoe lace. Next, staple the cut-out with the yarn on top of the other cut-out, creating a "pocket" in the shoe. Stuff the shoes with candy, stickers, pencils, or other small treats and hide them around the room. Let each student take a turn finding a present. When a student has found a present, have him reveal his present to the class, then let another student try. Continue until each student has found a present.

Australia Day

On January 26, 1788, Captain Arthur Phillip and the First Fleet arrived at Sydney, Australia and formed the first permanent European settlement on the continent. Today, many Australians celebrate this anniversary by giving awards, watching fireworks, and holding barbecues with friends and family.

Crocodile Cards

The European settlers were introduced to many of the native animals of Australia, such as the kangaroo, koala, bilby, platypus, dingo, and crocodile! Let students "bite" into Australia Day with these crocodile cards! Have each student cut a crocodile mouth out of green poster board. Then, have students cut the mouths in half. Cut small white triangles from poster board and have each student glue several of them along the bottom of the top mouth piece to resemble teeth. Next, have each student draw an eye on the top of the crocodile head. Attach the top and bottom pieces together with a paper fastener to create a hinge. Have students cut out small squares of poster board, write Australia Day messages on them, such as *Happy Australia Day, Long Live Australia*, etc., and glue them to the backs of their crocodile mouths. When the crocodile mouth is opened, the Australia Day message will be revealed!

Happy Australia Day!

G'day, Mate!

In honor of Australia Day, teach the class some Australian lingo and have them draw literal pictures of the phrases.

Laughing Gear = mouth
Dial = face
Happy as Larry = fortunate or lucky
Silly Season = summer holiday between December and Australia Day
Score a Bait = receive an invitation
Chew the Fat = talk

Have students write the phrases they have drawn on the backs of their pictures. As each student shares his picture with the class, let others guess which Australian phrase he has illustrated.

Australian of the Year

Awards are given on Australia Day as part of the festivities. Winners of the Australian of the Year, Young Australian of the Year, Senior Australian of the Year, Community of the Year, and Young Achievers are announced. Hold a class Australian of the Year celebration! Provide reference materials on famous Australians, such as Nancy Bird, John Flynn, Truganini, Edith Cowan, and Evonne Goolagong Cawley. Have students choose a candidate, write a short report on why that person should be named Australian of the year, and design a medal for that person.

Have each student present her report and medal to the class. Hang the reports and medals on a bulletin board titled *Australians of the Year.*

Australian of the Year
Evonne Goolagong Cawley